Theologies of Power and Crisis

American Society of Missiology Monograph Series

The ASM Monograph Series provides a forum for publishing quality dissertations and studies in the field of missiology. Collaborating with Pickwick Publications—a division of Wipf and Stock Publishers of Eugene, Oregon—the American Society of Missiology selects high quality dissertations and other monographic studies that offer research materials in mission studies for scholars, mission and church leaders, and the academic community at large. The ASM seeks scholarly work for publication in the Series that throws light on issues confronting Christian world mission in its cultural, social, historical, biblical, and theological dimensions.

Missiology is an academic field that brings together scholars whose professional training ranges from doctoral-level preparation in areas such as scripture, history and sociology of religions, anthropology, theology, international relations, interreligious interchange, mission history, inculturation, and church law. The American Society of Missiology, which sponsors this series, is an ecumenical body drawing members from Independent and Ecumenical Protestant, Catholic, Orthodox, and other traditions. Members of the ASM are united by their commitment to reflect on and do scholarly work relating to both mission history and the present-day mission of the church. The ASM Monograph Series aims to publish works of exceptional merit on specialized topics, with particular attention given to work by younger scholars, the dissemination and publication of which is difficult under the economic pressures of standard publishing models.

Persons seeking information about the ASM or the guidelines for having their dissertations considered for publication in the ASM Monograph Series should consult the Society's website: www.asmweb.org.

Members of the ASM Monograph Committee who approved this book are:

Paul V. Kollman, CSC, University of Notre Dame
Roger Schroeder, SVD, Catholic Theological Union
Michael A. Rynkiewich, Asbury Theological Seminary

Previously published in the ASM Monograph Series:

Ken Christoph Miyamoto
God's Mission in Asia: A Comparative and Contextual Study of This-Worldly Holiness and the Theology of Missio Dei in M. M. Thomas and C. S. Song

Edley J. Moodley
Shembe, Ancestors, and Christ: A Christological Inquiry with Missiological Implications

Roberta R. King
Pathways in Christian Music Communication: The Case of the Senufo of Cote d'Ivoire

E. Paul Balisky
Wolaitta Evangelists: A Study of Religious Innovation in Southern Ethiopia, 1937–1975

W. Jay Moon
African Proverbs Reveal Christianity in Culture: A Narrative Portrayal of Builsa Proverbs Contextualizing Christianity in Ghana

Auli Vahakangas
Christian Couples Coping with Childlessness: Narratives from Machame, Kilimanjaro

David J. Endres
American Crusade: Catholic Youth in the World Mission Movement from World War l through Vatican ll

Colleen Mary Mallon
Traditioning Disciples: The Contributions of Cultural Anthropology to Ecclesial Identity

Christopher L. Flanders
About Face: Rethinking Face for 21st Century Mission

Theologies of Power and Crisis
Envisioning/Embodying Christianity in Hong Kong

STEPHEN C. PAVEY

With a Foreword by Darrell L. Whiteman

American Society of Missiology
Monograph Series

10

☙PICKWICK *Publications* • Eugene, Oregon

THEOLOGIES OF POWER AND CRISIS
Envisioning/Embodying Christianity in Hong Kong

American Society of Missiology Monograph Series 10

Copyright © 2011 Stephen C. Pavey. All rights reserved. Except for brief quotations in critical publications or reviews, no part of this book may be reproduced in any manner without prior written permission from the publisher. Write: Permissions, Wipf and Stock Publishers, 199 W. 8th Ave., Suite 3, Eugene, OR 97401.

Revised Standard Version of the Bible, copyright © 1952 [2nd edition, 1971] by the Division of Christian Education of the National Council of the Churches of Christ in the United States of America. Used by permission. All rights reserved.

Pickwick Publications
An Imprint of Wipf and Stock Publishers
199 W. 8th Ave., Suite 3
Eugene, OR 97401

www.wipfandstock.com

ISBN 13: 978-1-60899-513-4

Cataloguing-in-Publication data:

Pavey, Stephen C.

Theologies of power and crisis : envisioning/embodying Christianity in Hong Kong / Stephen C. Pavey.

xvi + 132 pp. ; 23 cm. Includes bibliographical references.

American Society of Missiology Monograph Series 10

ISBN 13: 978-1-60899-513-4

1. Christianity—Hong Kong. 2. Power (Christian Theology). I. Title. II. Series.

BR1288 P25 2011

Manufactured in the U.S.A.

In loving memory of,
Dr. Robert William Lyon, Sr., a.k.a. Bob

Power remains the most important theological and ethical issue facing the Western church and thus far that church has not, except for a few voices, faced it in any radically honest way . . . a larger part of the problem is the fact that power is so obviously effective and useful. Its utilitarian value cannot be questioned.

—Bob Lyon, *The Poor Church as the Truly Evangelic Church*

Contents

Foreword by Darrell L. Whiteman / *xi*

Acknowledgments / *xv*

1 Entrée into the Field / 1

2 Overview / 5

3 Descriptive Integration / 41

4 Unholy Alliance—Theologies of Dominance and Crisis / 61

5 Prophetic Imagination—Theological Alternatives to Power / 82

6 Conclusions / 100

Afterword by John van Willigen / 113

Bibliography / 117

Foreword

IN 1992 MY FAMILY and I spent a sabbatical living in Hong Kong researching the development of indigenous churches and the cross-cultural adjustment of American missionaries. It was a thrilling and exciting time living in this vibrant city, discovering how Christianity was connecting with the concerns of Hong Kong Chinese. Two observations stood out. Christians were numbered primarily among the middle and upper-middle class in contrast to the poor, and there was a mass exodus of pastors fleeing Hong Kong in anticipation of the "communist takeover" when Hong Kong would revert back to China in 1997 from its status as a British colony.

I remember how frustrated I was with these pragmatic pastors concerned for their own survival abandoning their flocks to head for greener pastures in Vancouver, San Francisco, and other major cities with a significant Chinese Diaspora. I wondered, "Why did this Hong Kong Christianity look so westernized and middle class, and why were the poor and oppressed so often ignored by these churches?" Now I'm beginning to understand what I observed, thanks to Steve Pavey's anthropological research.

By viewing the 1997 Crisis, as it was commonly called, through the lens of political-economic processes and realities, and seeing more clearly the role of structural power in social relationships and religion, we get a quite different and sobering perspective on the dominant role of the Christian church in Hong Kong society.

This leads me to ask, what happens when the teachings of Jesus which were so much on the side of the poor and the oppressed, become wedded with institutions, denominational structures, and Christian programs that are entangled with power, prestige, and position? In contrast to Jesus' ministry, Christian theology and ideology can be used to legitimize an oppressive social order instead of used to liberate those who are oppressed. The problem is that as long as our churches are growing, and our missions are expanding their influence, we think that all is well in heaven and on earth, and so we seldom question the impact of our methods or motives on our mission. Well, this study of Christianity in Hong Kong is a wake up call. Perhaps it took a Christian missiological anthropologist to sound the alarm. Drawing on anthropologist Eric Wolf's political-economic theories of how ideas and power converge, Pavey has written a delightful ethnohistorical case study of Christianity in Hong Kong in the midst of dramatic change.

It is now common place to recognize that culture shapes our theologies, but if we dig a little deeper, and go a little further in our research we'll discover that power is also very much at work in shaping the ways we think about God, and envision living as Christians. While we may be quick to see the hand of culture, we're hesitant to admit the role of structural power in creating our theologies that in turn can so easily be used to legitimize inequality. Hong Kong gives us a good case study of an "Unholy Alliance" where the business interests are served by the government and morally sanctioned by the church. Pavey demonstrates how the institutional church follows in line after big business and the executive government. He notes that the theologies of largely middle-class, western educated Hong Kong Christians, focus on private spiritual interests in order to maintain economic prosperity and political stability. He says, "The Christian message in Hong Kong is understood as relevant to only the private or spiritual dimension of life allowing for the ideology and values associated with laissez-faire economics to rule the public dimensions of life. The church stays away from political and economic issues for the sake of stability and prosperity." But there is another side to this story.

Culture is always contested and contingent, and so is Christianity in Hong Kong. There is a minority voice, mainly among the parachurch organizations that advocates for the poor and oppressed and envisions the role of the church in responding to their needs instead of justifying its relationship with power. Pavey says that this minority group of Christians, "contest the meaning and practice of Christianity by resisting the structural and organizational power of the dominant church and society especially over the meaning and place of the poor in Hong Kong society. These minority Christians envision and embody Christian mission as largely one of crossing economic boundaries rather than the traditional view of crossing ethnic boundaries."

Pavey says, "I hope this case study of Hong Kong Christianity will contribute to better understanding of Christianities in order to reshape more just forms of Christian practice and relations of power." In my judgment, Pavey has done that and more. Until recently anthropology and theology have kept their distance, but in the last 10-15 years a new genus of anthropological studies has emerged that looks at the anthropology of Christianity. This book is a worthy contributor to that growing and important body of literature.

Missiology will gain much from critiques by sympathetic anthropologists who call us back to the teachings of Jesus in mission. Noting a growing gap between the church culture and the grass-roots culture, Pavey quotes Agnes Liu who says, "Too often, conversion to Christ becomes conversion to middle-class values and lifestyle because this is the dominant culture of the church in Hong Kong." Although Pavey's study is mostly about structural power, in explaining why Christianity in Hong takes the form that it does, he has avoided the mistake of reducing all causal explanations to simply power issues. He has a balanced and integrated approach to understanding the role of structural power in shaping ideas and practices within the Christian church and demonstrates that power is interdependent with ideas in shaping social relations.

Toward the conclusion of his book Pavey asserts that "Questioning certainties will certainly not endear one to the missiological communities but it must be done." I agree that it must be done but I disagree that it won't be welcomed. We need more of this kind of scrutiny, not less, but it will require that we relinquish our need for certainty in exchange for our quest for understanding. May God give us the wisdom and courage to do so.

Darrell L. Whiteman
Vice-President for Mission Personnel & Preparation
and Resident Missiologist
The Mission Society

Acknowledgments

I owe my deepest gratitude to Luella, my loving partner. She has been my loyal "Sam," who sacrificially walked every mile of this book's journey, helping carry "Frodo's" burden. The research and work represented by this book is deeply indebted to Luella's loving commitment to embody these words, "Come on, Mr. Frodo. I can't carry it for you, but I can carry you."

1

Entrée into the Field

JULY 1, 1997—THE HONG KONG HANDOVER

A BLACK ROLLS ROYCE pulled up in front of the Mandarin Oriental Hotel, the luxury hotel situated along Victoria Harbor on Hong Kong Island located in the middle of Hong Kong's big business district. My wife and I stood just outside with several friends waiting on a mutual friend from Taiwan to close a deal in the hotel's cigar lounge on the opening of a new bar in the expensive mid levels district. Fancy cars had been pulling up for the last hour to escort the privileged guests to the newly built Hong Kong Convention and Exhibition Centre not far away in Wanchai where they would participate in the handover events only a few hours away. I jokingly said to my friends, "get your cameras ready, the next person to come out will be Margaret Thatcher." They laughed. But seconds later our laughter turned to gasps when none other than Lady Thatcher emerged from the entrance, just a hand shake from where we stood, and was quickly whisked away in the black Rolls. The excitement of the handover ceremonies was just beginning.

We had come to Hong Kong with one million other visitors including eight thousand registered journalists and photographers to witness with the 6.5 million Hong Kong residents the return of Hong Kong to her motherland. On July 1st, 1997, China would resume sovereignty over Hong Kong after 156 years of British control. Britain would hand over the New Territories, whose ninety-nine-year lease had expired, as well as Kowloon and Hong Kong Island, land that had been acquired through the "unequal treaties" of 1842 and 1860. According to the Sino-British Joint Declaration worked out in December 1984 between Margaret Thatcher and Deng Xiaoping, China guaranteed a "high degree of autonomy" for

Hong Kong people in all matters "except in foreign and defense affairs" under Deng's "one country, two systems" policy. "Hong Kong's previous capitalist system and life-style shall remain unchanged for fifty years" (Joint Declaration 1984 and Basic Law 1989). Although no "significant" change was to occur, the world's spotlight was now focused on Hong Kong. Why? The flags of other European powers had been lowered on many other colonies before. This handover, however, was unique in several ways.

Politically, Hong Kong, unlike most other colonies who gained independence, would be transferred from a Western sovereign, who advocated democracy (under Christopher Patten's leadership), to an authoritarian state, the People's Republic of China. Could the Hong Kong handover process be better characterized as re-colonization rather than de-colonization? Economically, as one of the world's richest and major financial centers, Hong Kong would be returned to a much poorer sovereign who was just beginning to experiment with free market economies. How would China treat its "golden egg?" Would Hong Kong eventually fall in the shadows of Shanghai? Socially, Hong Kong is an open, global, and multifarious space that now faced the reality of a return to a motherland that hesitates little to intrude into community and individual's private lives. The June 4, 1989, Tiananmen incident poignantly awakened the Hong Kong people to their love of China's people and at the same time to the values they cherished as Hong Kong people. This is why we were all there. We were waiting to see what it would mean politically, economically, and socially to live in "one country" under "two systems."

Shortly after we caught a glimpse of Margaret Thatcher, our friend returned. Despite misty and cloudy weather, we hurried up the peak to the Government House so we could see Governor Patten and his family bid farewell to their home of five years. From the Mandarin Oriental we made our way slowly through Statue Square and the maze of thousands of Filipino female migrants, most who work as domestic servants, gathered in hundreds of small groups to eat, chat, sing, and dance. I wondered what Hong Kong's future held for them. Passing under the high tech computer controlled Hong Kong and Shanghai Bank that looks something like a space ship, we followed a narrow path that cut through the gardens next to St. John's Cathedral, a very traditional colonial structure built in 1847. We oriented our path in relation to the second largest building in Hong Kong, the modern triangular Bank of China designed by I. M. Pei, which stands seventy-four floors high just to the east of the Government House. The closer we got to the Patten residence, the larger the crowd became. We eventually came to an abrupt stop sandwiched in between people and tall buildings. There was a great deal of excitement in the air. Finally, a cheer went up from the crowd and we caught a brief glimpse of the Governor's car on its way to the Convention Centre after just making its triple trip around the home for good-luck, according to local belief, to ensure that the departing person would return again safely. The crowd rushed forward, carrying us along, to attempt an entrance into the official residence. Instead, we were met by a frustrated police force who had formed a human chain and threatened, through a megaphone, to resort to violence if necessary. We dispersed as quickly as possible.

The farewell ceremonies were just about to begin anyway. These ceremonies, long planned for at Hong Kong's tallest and most expensive venues, would largely be restricted to a list of invitees and the press. My wife Luella and I managed to make one of those lists for a dinner party on the top of the YMCA building, one of the highest vantage points on the Kowloon side of Victoria harbor across from Hong Kong Island. We managed this through *guanxi* (connections) with a friend whose father was on the board of directors of the YMCA Salisbury Hotel. After a delicious meal, we made our way out onto the roof with the other dignitaries to watch the HK$3.9 million fireworks display. It was a fantastic one-hour pyrotechnic extravaganza of nearly twenty thousand explosions over Victoria Harbor against the backdrop of one of the world's most dramatic cityscapes of Hong Kong Island. The natural beauty of Victoria Peak at 522 meters rises just above the hundreds of tall sky skyscrapers, now decorated with colorful lights that hug the crowded shoreline of the island. A crowd of over 420 thousand people pressed shoulder to shoulder in the streets below along the waterfront as we mingled with the VIP guests dressed in black tie attire sipping champagne in comfort. The loud booms, bright colors, and fantastic scene shook and marveled the crowd. President Jiang Zemin, Premier Li Peng, Prince Charles, and Governor Patten all were waiting just across the river in the Convention center for the handover ceremonies that were to begin at 11:00 p.m.

After the fireworks, we joined the massive crowds below in the streets of Tsimshatsui where the festivity and craziness of the occasion was much more intense. Hong Kong's main tourist district, usually filled with the hustle and bustle of shopping, now hosted the chaotic festivities of the handover celebration. We joined this dizzying sea of humanity in its slow movement through the closed-off streets of Tsimshatsui and into the numerous MTR (subway) stations to return home to our television sets. We returned to our temporary residence, the home of a Taiwanese family, just in time to watch the end of the official handover ceremony. The mood was solemn on TV. I could only make out parts of the conversation in Mandarin Chinese our host family was having around us. I certainly could not miss that they were making fun of Jiang's speech and the way that he and the Chinese officials would clap for themselves every few minutes. At midnight, Governor Patten and his family along with Prince Charles boarded the royal yacht Britannia to begin their journey home, formally ending the 156 years of British rule in Hong Kong.

This snapshot tourist peek into the handover events discloses little more than what the world saw on television. It does not easily reveal the changes that have taken place since the signing of the Joint Declaration in 1984 or the changes that will occur over the next fifty years. This more complex picture of Hong Kong particularly of the place of Christianity is what I hope I captured in this research when I returned after the handover events.

2

Overview

At this millennial transition, the human capacity to envision imaginary worlds seems to be shifting into high gear. For anthropologists and others, greater concern with how ideas and power converge seems eminently warranted.

—Eric Wolf, *Envisioning Power*

INTRODUCTION

THE RESEARCH IN THIS book follows the directive of Eric Wolf in *Envisioning Power* to better understand the relationship of ideas and power grounded in case study research. I use the perceived crisis of the "1997 handover" of Hong Kong to Mainland China (1982–1997) as a case study to explore "the relations of power that are played out in social arrangements and cultural configurations, and to trace out the possible ways in which these relations of power implicate ideas" (Wolf 1999, 3). This research pursues two primary questions: How did Hong Kong Christians respond ideationally in theological terms to the perceived crisis and how were these ideas and the actions based on them embedded in material and historical processes of structural power?

More specifically, this research seeks to explain what Wolf calls the "problem of cosmology" or the problem of "imaginary worlds" by investigating the theological processes of the Hong Kong Christian community (1999, 280–81). I am concerned with understanding how theological discourses and practices "engage with the material resources and organizational arrangements they try to affect or transform" (1999, 280). How the Hong Kong Christian community creates and experiences Christianity—socially, politically, and economically is a problem I explore as an attempt to understand how power and ideas connect through the social domain of theology. The research examines the theological discourses and practices as a contested dynamic dialectical process of meaning making and power wielding. This research demonstrates both how structural relations of power legitimize and constrain theological discourse and practice on the one hand and on the other how theological agency may also resist power relations that legitimize exploitation and injustice. This work begins what might be called a political economy of theological practice. It is normative to think of power in terms of political and economic processes. However, when we think of theology, power is rarely implicated as significant to the discussion. This study links theologies to political and economic processes in terms of historical and structural relations of power. This study will contribute to a better understanding of the role theological discourse and practice play in politics and economics, as well as contributing to a broader understanding of the relationship between power (material) and ideas (symbolic).

Ethnographically, this research situates itself in Hong Kong during the period that marks the return of Hong Kong to China. The geographic location and historic context provide a context of significant perceived crisis and culture change within which to study the response of Hong Kong Christians. The year 1982 marks an important shift in theological practice for Hong Kong Christians when formal talks began between Britain and China over how to handle the July 1, 1997, terminus of a ninety-nine year lease on the New Territories. This research examines the relationship between Hong Kong Christianity and the reshaping of structural relations of power. Christian organizations played a significant role in shaping Hong Kong's history and socio-cultural environment. This research examines the ongoing influence and changing roles of the Christian community in the broader Hong Kong context as well as the political, economic, and social implications of the change of sovereignty on the local Hong Kong Chinese Christian population.

On July 1, 1997, China resumed sovereignty over Hong Kong after 156 years of British control making it the Hong Kong Special Administrative Region of the People's Republic of China (HKSAR). The viability of Hong Kong poses concerns not only for local residents but also for wider regional and international interests in Mainland China, Taiwan, the Pacific Rim, and western multinational corporations. China's administrative policies promise stability and no "significant" changes. According to the Sino-British Joint Declaration worked out in December

1984 between Margaret Thatcher and Deng Xiaoping, China guarantees a "high degree of autonomy" for Hong Kong people in all matters "except in foreign and defense affairs" following Deng's "one country, two systems" policy. Hong Kong's previous capitalist system and life-style are to remain unchanged for fifty years (Joint Declaration 1984 and Basic Law 1989). Of particular interest to this research project, the Sino-British Joint Declaration (1984) and the Basic Law (1989, article 32, 141) both stipulate that Hong Kong's religious freedoms will be protected based on the principles of "non-subordination, non-interference, and mutual respect." Yet, the implementation of these policies in practice poses real challenges to local Hong Kong Chinese communities (Ma 1997; Siu 1997; Chan 1998; Choi 1998; Man and Lo 1998; Feng 1998).

This proposed research seeks to better comprehend the interplay of cultural and material forms of social life by focusing on the political, economic, and social implications of this change of sovereignty on the theological discourse and practice of local Hong Kong Chinese Christians. This community is of particular interest for several reasons: (1) the long and significant history of Christianity within the unique colonial situation of Hong Kong and the China region, (2) it's local significance concerning relations of power and the complicity between church, government and business communities, and (3) it's theoretical significance connecting power and ideas and further theology with political-economy studies.

Finally, it would be a mistake to understand the problems this research addresses as innocuous theoretical problems pertinent only for academic purposes. This would belie the urgency and potency of the problems faced by humanity today concerning destructive maladaptive human behavior that is legitimized through sacred ideologies and sanctified authorities. I view anthropology along with Wolf as a "critical tool with which to address social concerns" that could be "used to create a better world" (2001, 2, 8). Out of a desire to ameliorate social suffering, Wolf studies the problematic relationship between power and ideas, especially in *Envisioning Power*, and for similar reasons I follow his research directive. As Wolf puts it, "there is a crucial link, to be understood much better than we do now, between interest and morality" (2001, 165). I agree with Aihwa Ong that we have a "moral obligation to understand how power relations work" (Ong 1995). Again, Wolf says, "We stand at the end of a century marked by colonial expansion, world wars, revolutions, and conflicts over religion that have occasioned great social suffering and cost millions of lives. These upheavals have entailed massive plays and displays of power, but ideas have had a central role in all of them. Ideas have been used to glorify or criticize social arrangements ..." (1999, 1). I am interested in going beyond description and interpretation in an attempt to seek explanations in order to address social concerns facing humanity that involve Christendom and religion. Roy Rappaport challenges me to do "engaged" anthropology or engage in "The Anthropology of Trouble" (1993; 1994). This research explores then the "pathologies" of Christian theologies (Rappaport 1999) in order to write against the sanctification of discourse and practice that exploit the powerless and protect structural relations of power that benefit the powerful. This research embraces a critical anthropological perspective to expose the contradictions of ecclesiastical hegemonies in Hong Kong that appear to be accepted by the society as natural and inviolable.

Eric Wolf states well the central problem that I bring to this research project. Concerning "systems of symbolic action," there is truth in the notion that they can be "mechanisms of domination and exploitation." Yet "there is also concrete truth in the notion advanced by others that systems of religious belief and practice can be modes of resistance against conquerors and exploiters. What we have not yet done systematically is to look at the multiplicity of symbolic actions as ideology, as expressions of different interests and aspirations embodied in cultural forms" (2001[1986], 164–165). Christian theologies have been used at different times and different places for both legitimizing and criticizing social arrangements that exploit and dominate the powerless. How does this happen when such diametrically opposed theological ideas and practices claim truths based on the same Bible, same God, and same history? How does Christianity manifest itself as both ecclesiastical hegemony and prophetic (critical) imagination?

These are important questions that the research directive and theoretical framework of Eric Wolf will help elucidate. For too long, both theologians and anthropologists have retreated to extreme positions that help us little with finding an answer. Any narrow view that imagines Christianity either as a wholly negative globalizing force or as the only true force for morality in the world has misunderstood the nature of religion, Christianity, and culture. Wolf helps us with this impasse by avoiding easy reductive answers and grounding his concern with the relationship of ideas and power in case study research. I hope this case study of Hong Kong Christianity will contribute to better understandings of Christianities in order to reshape more just forms of Christian practice and relations of power.

BRIEF STATEMENT OF THE PROBLEM

This research examines the theological responses of Hong Kong Chinese Christians during a period of significant social change and perceived crisis inaugurated by the Sino-British Joint Declaration (1982–1984), proceeding through the transition of Hong Kong to a Special Administrative Region of Mainland China (1997) to the current "post-colonial" reality. The research focuses on the dialectical interpenetration between these theological ideas and practices and the historical and material forms of social life.

THEMES

Several important themes emerge from the research and interweave themselves through the development of the dissertation. First, the research demonstrates that the structural relations of power that control and legitimize Hong Kong's local-global economy are political and economic as well as historical, cultural, and moral. That is, the structural fields of power are defined by more than just the flow of commodities, the accumulation of capital, or access to labor. There are also flows of values and ideas that serve to legitimize as well as challenge the making and unmaking of structural relations of power (Wolf 1999; Appadurai 1996). "Capitalism, no less than Christianity, depends on formation processes to sustain itself in the world; making people 'fit for capitalism' is no less important to the workings of the world economy than processes of production, distribution, and finance" (Budde and Brimlow 2000, 61). As Wolf says it, "Power was thus made to depend not merely on 'production' (the active interchange of humans with nature) and on 'society' (the normatively governed interactions among humans) but also on relationships with imaginary elements and beings projected beyond tangible experiences into metaphysical worlds" (Wolf 1999, 281).

The perspective of Christianity that emerges from this study of Hong Kong Christian ideas and their embodiment in practice reveals a domain of social practice that is contested, complex, and dynamic.

Christian representations reveal a flexibility shaped by competing interests across social domains and within a political-economic context. These theologies cannot be reduced to material processes but neither can they be removed. Theological representations are always embedded in the historical and material processes of life including economics, politics, ecology, social organization, and plays of power. The formation of Hong Kong Christians requires the reciprocal construction of practices across social domains within the processes of capital accumulation. The relevance of Christian theologies are always embedded in the historical particularities of a political-economic context in terms of the meaning they purport, the power they assert, and the relations they legitimize.

Although the vision and practice of Christianity is contested, Christianity overall in Hong Kong supports a vision that promotes the interests of business elites, promulgates neo-liberal values, and acquiesces to the authority of Beijing. Christian discourse and practice might be said to be "capital-friendly" for the dominant practice of Christianity has played an important part as a moral authority that guards the values inherent in this system. Emily Lau described these relations of power as an "unholy alliance" where business interests in Hong Kong are served by the government and morally sanctioned by the church (Lau 1987, 23). Yet, there is also, on the margins, a minority of Christians whose discourse and practice challenge this unholy alliance and represent a struggle over the practice, meaning, and representation of Christianity. Their responses of resistance vary from advocating for human rights and democracy to the inclusion of those most marginal into their own communities. At the center of their theological practice and discourse is a critique (sometimes implicit) of the structural relations legitimized by the dominant values of the free market system. The research shows that Christian discourse and practice may serve to legitimize the ideologies of dominance as well as serve as a "moral" force for social justice.

ZONES OF THEORIZING

A local anthropologist and friend treated me to lunch at the New Asia College café where we met to discuss my research project. Chinese University's anthropology department, located within New Asia College, was where my friend worked. The Chinese University of Hong Kong helped with my residence requirements by making me a visiting scholar. I asked him what he thought about my choice of research subject and topic. He found the topic both interesting and relevant to the anthropology of Hong Kong. He said, "The anthropological research community in Hong Kong has stayed away from studying the church as a social institution." Why, I asked. It was difficult for him to locate an answer. "Maybe because it is just too difficult," he said. He agreed that Christianity played an important role in the social configuration of Hong Kong and now he wondered why the anthropology community dismissed it in their research on Hong Kong. His own parents were Catholic, and like most people who had achieved a relatively high level of social status in Hong Kong, he had attended schools run by Christian organizations. The topic was important especially given the lacunae within the research community. Throughout the period of my field research, he would become a source of encouragement and an advocate for the significance of my research topic.

The reasons for the difficulty in studying Christianity from an anthropological perspective are too varied and complex to explicate fully within the scope of this dissertation. However, I think it is important to identify possible detractors that appear to be inherent biases within our research community. This research addresses this "politics of place" in theorizing and attempts to move away from popular "zones of theorizing" within the field of anthropology on the subject of religion, especially of Christianity (Abu-Lughod 1989; Asad 1986). The research discovered early in the research process particular "gatekeeping concepts . . . that seem to limit anthropological theorizing about the place in question, and that define the quintessential and dominant questions of interest in the region" (Appadurai 1986, 357).

ANTHROPOLOGY AND HONG KONG

The anthropological study of Hong Kong did not begin until the early 1950s when Barbara Ward arrived to study the *Tanka* (boat people), a group marginal to Hong Kong society. As more anthropologists arrived to study Hong Kong through the 1950s and 1960s, they focused primarily on the rural villages of the New Territories in attempt to better understand the China that was closed to the world after 1949 (Potter; Groves; Topley; Baker; Freedman; Aijmer; Watson). It was a kind of salvage anthropology similar to the anthropological studies of Chinese society in Taiwan conducted during the same period. A few studies on urban and modernizing Hong Kong began in the 1970s (Blake 1981; Guldin 1977,

1982; Myers 1976, 1981; Salaff 1974, 1981), but they largely came to a halt by the early 1980s when China reopened and anthropologists moved across the border to study mainland China. Until recently, scholars interested in the "real" China have not taken Hong Kong seriously (Wong 1986, 324). An anthropology department was created in the 1980s at the Chinese University of Hong Kong, but their focus remained on minority groups and the stuff of "traditional" Chinese society. However, more recently, as a result of the 1997 handover, Hong Kong became increasingly an important site for research. The Hong Kong handover drew researchers from all over the world and from many different disciplines including political science, economics, history, cultural studies, missiology, and anthropology. The cultural identity of the *Heung Gong yahn* (Hong Kong people) emerged as a dominant theme for theorizing. Many studies examine the contested process of identity formation at the nexus of nationalism, ethnicity, gender, and modernization (Baker; Evans and Tam; Faure; Lilley; Mathews; Siu; Smart). Apart from anthropology, the dominant focus of research was on economic and political forecasting of Hong Kong's future.

This project began with an interest in the place of Christianity in Hong Kong. The hot issue was the construction, deconstruction, and meaning of cultural identities. Inevitably, the first question I began to pursue was the construction of Christian identities at the nexus of nation making and ethnicity. In April 2000, at the International Postgraduate Symposium on Hong Kong Culture and Society, a local anthropology student presented a paper on the topic of Hong Kong identities. A prominent local anthropologist challenged this student to clarify what he was presenting as new on the topic. There appeared to be a consensus in the discussion that followed that the topic of Hong Kong identity was "over researched" with little new theorizing. Arif Dirlik, keynote speaker for the conference, addressed the issue as a problem related to the meaning of culture. He suggested a "political-economic take on culture" as useful, that is, "how culture is shaped by the political-economy." Further, he suggested culture should be studied in terms of practice, that is, individuals are not only products of culture but also producers of culture. This is the direction I pursued in my research, but with a focus more on power, that is, the way in which relations of power impinge upon meaning and the process of identity formation. What I was adding to the discussion on identity was a focus on power and a focus on Christian theologizing.

It is normative to think of power in terms of political and economic processes. But when we think of theology, power is rarely implicated as significant to the discussion. I want to link theology to political and economic processes in terms of the exercise of power.

While anthropology within Hong Kong has been slow to study the effects of modernization, it has almost completely ignored the role of Christianity in affecting change and social relations in Hong Kong. There are a few exceptions: Nicole Constable studied a small village of marginalized Hakka Christians (1994), Agnes Liu studied a marginalized group of Hoklo Christians undergoing economic transformations (1999), and Chan Shun-hing studied a group of "grassroots" charismatic churches (1995). However, none of these studies aims at getting the macro-level picture of Christianity within its historical or political-economic context. The study of Christianity in Hong Kong by anthropologists is lacking in part because of the assumptions, practices, and biases within the larger anthropological community concerning religion and Christianity in particular. In the next section, I take up a discussion of these biases that lead anthropologists to exclude Christianity, particularly western manifestations, from the anthropological lens.

ANTHROPOLOGY AND RELIGION: A HISTORY VIA EVANS-PRITCHARD

I will trace a brief history of the anthropology of religion up to and through the writings of E. E. Evans-Pritchard (1902–1973) in order to provide a context for this work and current anthropological approaches to religion. Evans-Pritchard is an appropriate choice for several reasons. First, he had a tremendous impact on the development of the anthropology of religion. *Witchcraft, Oracles and Magic among the Azande* and *Nuer Religion* remain to this day classic ethnographic texts all anthropologists studying religion should be familiar with. In addition to the rich ethnographic texts he provided us with, he also made a significant theoretical contribution to our understanding of religion. His perception of the relationship between anthropology and religion is insightful and remains apt for today. I consider Evans-Pritchard the most significant figure in the anthropological study of religion standing between Durkheim and Geertz. He is important in part because his historical approach helps us move beyond Geertz.

In addition, he is important to my study for his challenge to the anthropological community regarding their bias against religion and unwillingness to explain it on its own terms rather than through modern scientific terms. Later, I will develop the theoretical perspective my study takes along with other current anthropologists that move us on to consider a political-economic approach to the study of religion and power. For now, this section examines the historical context of the anthropology of religion and at the same time does this by paying respect to Evans-Pritchard's important contribution. This history examines in particular the relationship between religion and anthropologists as the context for understanding his critique of former theories and the formation of new ones.

In order to better understand the contribution of Evans-Pritchard to the anthropology of religion, we need to place him in a historical context. Spencer, Tylor, Frazer, R. R. Marett, W. Robertson Smith, Durkheim, Mauss, Levy-Bruhl, Radcliffe-Brown, Freud, and Malinowski all contribute to the anthropology of religion to which Evans-Pritchard is reacting and responding to. I do not intend to trace the complete history of the anthropology of religion, but I rather hope to elucidate the broad theoretical streams of anthropological thought on religion. In *The Institutions of Primitive Society* (1956a), *Theories of Primitive Religion* (1965) and in a lecture entitled "Religion and the Anthropologists" (1972), Evans-Pritchard identifies and examines the theories that he views as significant to the history of the anthropology of religion. I find myself in agreement with Evans-Pritchard and therefore attempt to look at this history through his eyes. These theories can be categorized as evolutionary, psychological, and sociological theories. My aim will be to grasp how each deals with religion and how Evans-Pritchard interprets each as inadequate.

The anthropological study of religion began in the latter half of the nineteenth century with evolutionary theories of religion. They shared a common research interest in primitive societies and the search for human origins. "Like so much else in anthropology, the study of religious notions of primitive people arose within the context of evolutionary theory. In the nineteenth century, to think systematically about human affairs was to think historically—to seek out survivals of the most elementary forms and to trace the steps by which these forms subsequently developed" (Geertz 1968, 399). Their theory of religion was similar to their theory of other social phenomenon, which is to say it evolved from a simple and homogenous state to a more complex and heterogeneous one. Tylor, Spencer, and Frazer all represent this theoretical interest in tracing the evolutionary stages of religion. Evans-Pritchard also recognizes two of Tylor's students, Lang and Marett, as making significant contributions to evolutionary theories of religion.

E. B. Tylor (1832–1917) reduced primitive religion to a belief in spirits, "animism." He introduced this concept first in *The Religion of Savages* (1866) and in detail later in *Primitive Culture* (1871). "Tylor, the leading anthropologist in England . . . laid it down as an axiom that the idea of God is a late conception in human history, the product of a long development of animistic thought" (Evans-Pritchard 1956a, 2). Herbert Spencer (1820–1903), in a similar manner, reduced religion to a belief in ghosts or ancestor worship in *The Principles of Sociology* (1876–1896). And in *First Principles* (1862), Spencer introduced "the earliest philosophic exposition of the position known as agnosticism" (Trompf 1987, 5). James Frazer (1854–1941), building on Tylor's theory, posited that humans evolve from magic to religion to science. I would agree with Evans-Pritchard when he suggests that these men were influenced by the French philosopher Comte (1798–1857), who believed that humans evolved through three stages, the theological, the metaphysical, and the positive (Evans-Pritchard 1965, 27; 1972, 195). Basically, "Victorian anthropologists . . . imagined what could be the crudest and most materialistic form of some institution, custom, or belief in their own society and then postulated this as its earliest historical form" (Evans-Pritchard 1956a, 3).

What these three men, Tylor, Frazer, and Spencer, have in common is that they intellectualized their approach to the study of religion (Geertz 1968, 399; Sharpe 1987, 107; Evans-Pritchard 1956a, 3). That is, they understood primitive religion as a rational attempt to make sense of the world around them. In their final analysis, primitive religious belief was based on erroneous reasoning albeit logical reasoning (Evans-Pritchard 1965, 94). Their work has the final effect of depreciating the primitive's mind and religious belief. Spencer wrote that the primitive mind is "unspeculative, uncritical, incapable of generalizing, and with scarcely any notions save those yielded by the perceptions" (Spencer 1882, 344). Evans-Pritchard summarizes their theories, "Primitive man was thus represented as childish, crude, prodigal, and comparable to animals and imbeciles" (Evans-Pritchard 1965, 105).

Andrew Lang (1844–1912) disagreed with Tylor that the idea of God was a late idea. He believed there was sufficient evidence to show that monotheism preceded animism as the earliest form of primitive belief (Evans-Pritchard 1956a, 2). He interpreted animism as an evolutionary degeneration of monotheism. R. R. Marett (1866–1943) also disagreed with Tylor that animism was the earliest form of primitive religion. "Marett felt that Tylor's animism was too sophisticated an idea to be the origin of religion. Marett suggested animatism, a belief in impersonal supernatural forces (mana), preceded the creation of spirits" (Ember and Ember 1990, 281).

Evans-Pritchard criticizes these early theorists for making sweeping generalizations based on incomplete and unreliable data, brought to them by travelers, traders, and missionaries. "How well was this procedure satirized by Malinowski, to whom must go much credit for having outmoded by ridicule and example" this sort of inquiry (Evans-Pritchard 1965, 9). They were "armchair anthropologists . . . whose experience was restricted to their own culture and society, within that society a small class, and within that class to yet smaller group of intellectuals" (Evans-Pritchard 1965, 108). "The interpretations that satisfied the Victorian and Edwardian anthropologists now appear so lacking in understanding that we are surprised that anyone could even have thought them adequate" (Evans-Pritchard 1956a, 9).

Lucien Levy-Bruhl (1857–1939), a French philosopher and sociologist, pursued the evolutionary idea of a primitive mode of thought into the twentieth century. He really follows Durkheim historically and categorically, but I treat him here because he "sought to establish the existence of a primitive mentality" (Riviere 1987, 533). Evans-Pritchard devotes an entire section to the treatment of Levy-Bruhl in his *Theories of Primitive Religion* (1965). "No account of theories of primitive religion would be adequate which did not devote special and separate attention to Levy-Bruhl's voluminous writings on primitive mentality" (Evans-Pritchard 1965, 78).

In *Primitive Mentality* (1922) and in *How Natives Think* (1910), Levy-Bruhl argues for a qualitative difference between primitive thought and civilized thought. He calls this primitive mentality "pre-logical" or "magico-religious" and civilized thought "critical" (Riviere 1987, 533). In

The Soul of the Primitive (1927), Levy-Bruhl introduces the notion of "mystical participation," the reality that primitives operate within (Riviere 1987, 533). "Mystical participation" stands in contrast to the "laws of Aristotelian logical reasoning" (Geertz 1968, 404). Here is where Levy-Bruhl differs from Tylor, Spencer, and Frazer. For Levy-Bruhl, primitive religion is not logical, instead, it is based on strong emotional forces. "Primitive man was thus made to appear . . . as quite irrational, living in a mysterious world of doubts and fears, in terror of the supernatural and ceaselessly occupied in coping with it" (Evans-Pritchard 1965, 10). John Middleton suggests that Evans-Pritchard's *Witchcraft, Oracles, and Magic among the Azande* (1937) and his *Nuer Religion* (1956b) are responses respectively to Levy-Bruhl's writings on "pre-logical" primitive mentality and "mystical participation" (Middleton 1987, 198). I believe this to be true in the first instance. Evans-Pritchard writes that he hopes he has persuaded the reader of "the intellectual consistency of Zande notions" (1937, 540). But I am not convinced that *Nuer Religion* is primarily a response to Levy-Bruhl as much as it is a response to the functionalist theories that we will examine later.

There were two major responses to the evolutionary theories of religion, the psychological and the sociological. Both responses move from an emphasis on seeking the origin of religion to understanding its function. Those supporting psychological theories believed humans were "guided by appetites and emotions rather than by reason" (Evans-Pritchard 1956a, 4). Further, they believed that religion functioned to satisfy human needs. Later, we will see how the sociological theories supported a different kind of functional analysis.

Sigmund Freud (1856–1939) and "his psychoanalytic insights have exerted a crucial influence on ideas about the psychological nature of religion" (Lessa and Vogt 1979, 2). In *Totem and Taboo*, he posited that "the beginnings of religion, ethics, society, and art meet in the Oedipus complex" (Freud 1938, 872). Basically, Freud believed that religion existed because of people's unresolved grief that leads to a fear of God. "For Freud it was comparable to obsessional neurosis, the product of wish fulfillment and the father complex" (Evans-Pritchard 1972, 199). He believed these religious beliefs were just a "phase of immaturity" that people would eventually outgrow (Evans-Pritchard 1956a, 5).

Malinowski (1884–1942), unlike Freud, interpreted religion in terms of its positive benefits. Malinowski believed that religion met basic needs of individuals in a culture. Fundamentally, religion functioned as a way of reducing anxiety (Evans-Pritchard 1965, 40–48, 94). "Religion arises and functions in situations of emotional stress, and particularly during the crises of life, such as initiation and death" (Evans-Pritchard 1956a, 5). Through religion, "man affirms his convictions that death is not real nor yet final, that man is endowed with a personality which persists over death..." (Malinowski 1939, 959). Evans-Pritchard did not spend a great deal of time discussing these theories because "evidence was seldom cited in support" of their theories (Evans-Pritchard 1956a, 5). "Durkheim and his colleagues and pupils of the *Annee Sociologique* (Hubert, Mauss, and Hertz) have steadfastly, and in my opinion rightly, opposed any such psychological explanations of religion" (Evans-Pritchard 1956a, 5).

Sociological theories of religion share in common a view that religion is a reflection of society. Like psychological theories, it was not important to look for the origin of religion. What was important was to study its function and structure.

Emile Durkheim (1858–1917), a monumental figure in the anthropology of religion, represents a bridge from evolutionary theory to a sociological-functional theory of religion. Influenced by W. Robertson Smith (1846–1894), Durkheim "treated religion . . . as typifying earlier stages of social development and 'mechanical solidarity'" (Lukes 1987, 517; Geertz 1968, 400; Evans-Pritchard 1965, 56). He was not interested in first origins like Tylor, Spencer, and Frazer. Instead, he wanted to discover "the ever-present causes upon which the most essential forms of religious thought and practice depend" (Durkheim 1915, 8). For Durkheim, "Religion is a social fact . . . being in the simpler societies bound up with other social facts, law, economics, art, etc., which later separate out from it and lead their own independent existences. Above all it is the way in which a society sees itself as more than a collection of individuals, and by which it maintains its solidarity and ensures its continuity" (Evans-Pritchard 1965, 56).

In *The Elementary Forms of Religion* (1912), Durkheim's last major work, he defines religion in causal, interpretative and functional terms (Lukes 1987, 518). First, he argues that religion is socially determined. "Men collectively invent the basic categories of religion in order to explain the unseen but felt force of the collective consciousness" (Harris 1968, 478). "For Durkheim, God is society" (Evans-Pritchard 1965, 63). It is on this causal explanation of religion that we will see that Evans-

Pritchard departs from Durkheim. Secondly, Durkheim argues that religion represents a social reality. Religious facts are social facts. They are "a way of symbolizing and dramatizing social relationships" (Lukes 1987, 518). Religion for Durkheim becomes a vehicle for interpreting meaning, specifically the meaning of the individual's place in the social reality. Lastly, Durkheim argues that religion functions to maintain the social order.

Evans-Pritchard admits that he is indebted a great deal to Durkheim's theories. He writes, "I would, though with serious reservations, identify myself with the Annee School if a choice had to be made and an intellectual allegiance declared" (Evans-Pritchard 1960, 24). Although there is much in common between Evans-Pritchard and Durkheim, we cannot ignore these "serious reservations." Evans-Pritchard's theory of religion is not influenced by Durkheim's functionalism in terms of causality, but rather as a theory that seeks to understand the "relation of parts to one another within a coherent system, each part making sense only in relation to other institutional systems" (Evans-Pritchard 1965, 112). Evans-Pritchard did not think religion could be reduced to social explanations. "I hold that it is not sound scientific method to seek for origins, especially when they cannot be found. Science deals with relations, not with origins and essences" (Evans-Pritchard 1965, 111). It is important to note that he does not deny that social forces exercise considerable influence over religious ideas.

One of Evans-Pritchard's greatest criticisms of Durkheim is the charge of "biased atheism," and this contribution is still incredibly relevant to the current state of anthropological studies. Evans-Pritchard writes, "I think it is significant that Durkheim was a militant atheist, not just an unbeliever but a propagandist for unbelief . . . He had to find some sort of explanation of what is a universal phenomenon in both time and space, and could only do so in terms of the sociological metaphysic to which he had irretrievably committed himself" (Evans-Pritchard 1981, 157). "It was Durkheim and not the savages who made society into God" (Evans-Pritchard 1956b, 313). We will see in more detail how Evans-Pritchard's theory of religion differs from Durkheim when we examine his *Nuer Religion*. The point here that Evans-Pritchard makes is that it is dangerous to analyze another religion in terms of one's own theological assumptions and terms, including Durkheim's "militant atheist" theology.

Evans-Pritchard viewed Radcliffe-Brown as the "English Durkheimian" (Evans-Pritchard 1965, 74). A. R. Radcliffe-Brown (1881–1945) continued Durkheim's idea of social determinism. He "agreed with Durkheim's postulate that the main role (or function) of religion was to celebrate and sustain the norms upon which the integration of society depends" (Geertz 1968, 402). Religion, then, helped to maintain the social order as a whole by strengthening social solidarity (Radcliffe-Brown 1965, 165).

Before turning to Evans-Pritchard's theory of religion, let us look at how he viewed the relationship between anthropology and religion. It is important for two reasons. First, it is part of his criticism of most anthropological theory before him. Second, it shapes his own theory of religion and specifically influences his own work in *Nuer Religion*. This is an issue that Evans-Pritchard brings up in many of his works reflecting the importance it must have held for him (1956a; 1956b; 1965; 1972).

Evans-Pritchard believed that anthropology, from its beginnings in the nineteenth century, held a certain ambivalence towards the study of religion. In a lecture delivered at Oxford in 1959, Evans-Pritchard begins, "It might be of interest to you were I to discuss the attitude of sociologists, and social anthropologists in particular, towards religious faith and practice. It has been for the most part bleakly hostile" (Evans-Pritchard 1972, 193). "Almost all the leading anthropologists of my own generation would, I believe, hold that religious faith is total illusion" (Evans-Pritchard 1972, 199). The implication is that the beliefs of the anthropologist affect the study of religion. Regarding the nineteenth century anthropologists, he wrote, "Their animosity toward revealed religion was not inspired solely by love of truth but was also a reaction to dreariness of their religious upbringing" (1972, 201). "Those who give assent to the religious beliefs of their own people feel and think, and therefore also write, differently about the beliefs of other peoples from those who do not give assent to them" (1956b, vii).

> The non-believer seeks for some theory: biological, psychological, or sociological—which will explain the illusion; the believer seeks rather to understand the manner in which a people conceives of a reality and their relation to it. For both, religion is part of social life, but for the believer it has also another dimension. On this point I find myself in agreement with Schmidt in his confutation of Renan: if religion is essentially of the inner life, it follows that it

> can only be grasped from within ... There is but too much danger that the other (the non-believer) will talk of religion as a blind man might of colours, or one totally devoid of ear, of a beautiful musical composition. (Evans-Pritchard 1965, 121)

This is a concern and criticism that anthropologist Edith Turner continues to raise even today.

It is important to clarify a matter this raises before we go any further. Evans-Pritchard writes, "What I have said does not imply that the anthropologist has to have a religion of his own, and I think we should be clear on this point at the outset" (1965, 17). It might be relevant to note that Evans-Pritchard converted to Catholicism later in life in 1944. Here he distinguishes between three kinds of anthropologists. There is the anthropologist who is antagonistic toward religious belief who will not be able to understand the religion of another. This was the most common view held by anthropologists according to Evans-Pritchard. The second category is the anthropologist who is neutral and attempts to understand religion as a social institution from an outsider's point of view. I take this to be where most anthropologists working on religion today are. But the anthropologist who he thinks is best fit for understanding and studying religion is the one who holds religious beliefs. As much as I agree with Evans-Pritchard's concern to understand religion on its own terms, I disagree that the anthropologist best suited is the one with religious beliefs. Let me explain further.

Evans-Pritchard writes, "If we wish to seize the essential nature of what we are inquiring into we have to try to examine the matter from the inside" (Evans-Pritchard 1956b, 122). He argues that the early anthropologist's animosity toward religion negatively affected their theory of religion. This is the main point he makes that I do agree with. "It was precisely because so many anthropological writers did take up a theological position, albeit a negative and implicit one, that they felt that an explanation of primitive religious phenomena in causal terms was required" (1965, 17).

He further argues that a familiarity with religious belief will help the anthropologist get at more than just "a superficial understanding" of religion (1965, 17). He even goes so far as to suggest that exegesis, symbolic thought, and theology are disciplines that would greatly enhance the work of the anthropologist (1965, 14–17). I certainly agree with this as well, and hope that I confirm that point within this study given my own religious education. My own study of Christianity in Hong Kong is informed by an extensive study of Christian history, theology, and biblical exegesis.

Nuer Religion, his final work on the Nuer, is an attempt to analyze religion on terms that are not wholly reducible to social function. Here is where he fundamentally breaks from Durkheim and other theories of religion. Evans-Pritchard's theory of religion moves from a strictly functionalist theory of religion to one of meaning. Evans-Pritchard stands as a significant bridge, like Durkheim, in the history of the anthropology of religion. These two may be the most significant figures in the anthropological study of religion up to their day. *Nuer Religion* (1956b) is largely a criticism of the "functionalist reduction of religion to society" (Evens 1982, 383). "That Nuer religious thought and practices are influenced by their whole social life is evident from our study of them . . . But the Nuer conception of God cannot be reduced to, or explained by, the social order" (Evans-Pritchard 1956b, 320). This is the giant break that Evans-Pritchard makes with previous theories of religion. He is suggesting that Nuer religion should be studied as a system on its own.

This is the case I also make for the study of Christianity in Hong Kong. Evans-Pritchard summaries his presuppositions about religion: "I do not deny that people have reasons for their own beliefs—that they are rational; I do not deny that religious rites my be accompanied by emotional experiences, that feeling may even be an important element in their performance; and I certainly do not deny that religious ideas and practices are directly associated with social groups—that religion, whatever else it may be, is a social phenomenon. What I do deny is that it is explained by any of these facts, or all of them together" (Evans-Pritchard 1965, 111). I agree.

ANTHROPOLOGY AND THE PROBLEM OF CHRISTIANITY

This thrust into metaphysics is not easily accommodated by anthropological efforts to explain human doings as practical ways of obtaining practical results. This is so despite the fact that the transactions of people with imaginary beings are both observable and describable, in that people engage in behaviors they then talk about. We have sought not so much to engage the imaginary as to explain it away, reducing "the output of minds" to seemingly more basic substrates.

— Eric Wolf, *Envisioning Power*

Although anthropology is predisposed to cross-disciplinary approaches, anthropology and theology have kept their distance (Lienhardt 1968). I already noted that Evans-Pritchard observed in 1959 that the relationship between anthropologists and religion "has been for the most part bleakly hostile" (Evans-Pritchard 1972, 193). Raymond Firth comments, "The study of religion . . . has divided anthropologists more deeply than any other position" (Firth 1981, 582). Recently, Stephen Glazier observed that efforts to establish a religion section within the American Anthropological Association have been "highly contested, and many anthropologists of religion express concern that their subject area has become 'marginalized'" and further that "a prospective student might experience considerable difficulty in putting together a plan of study that focuses on the anthropology of religion" (Glazier 1997, 1). Asad criticizes anthropology further for its "dearth of work by anthropologists on Christianity" in particular (Asad 1983). "Modern anthropology . . . has rarely thought fit to address itself to Christian history, and in matters of this kind most anthropologists are at least as traditional as the societies they usually study" (Asad 1983, 238).

The work in the volume edited by Eric Wolf in 1991 was in part a response to this lacuna within the anthropology of religion. This new research perspective led early on by Mart Bax attempts to reconcile political and religious anthropology in order to explore the "mutual conditioning of processes of meaning and of power" by focusing the anthropological lens on Christian history and institutions (Bax 1991, 8). I will expand on the development of this research perspective in the next section as my own work builds upon the trajectory set by Asad, Bax, and Wolf. The point I make here is that although religion has been an important subject for anthropologist, the approach to understand it has been limited, one-sided, and marginalized especially with regards to the study of Christianity. I agree with Mary Douglas that this current problem is in part due to the cultural biases of the social scientists (Douglas 1982, 2–3; Bourdillon 1993, 1995; Poewe 1994; Harding 1987, 1991; Wagner 1997; Shaw 1995; Saler 1993; Stipe 1980; Glazier 2000; Ewing 1994; Goodman 1991; Bax 1991; 1993; Pandian 1991, 2001, 2002).

Much of this anthropological bias comes from anthropology's own embeddedness in modernity, including among other assumptions the inevitability of the secularization thesis. But recent studies reveal much the opposite of the secularization thesis and instead, demonstrate religion's vitality and roles in both oppression and resistance around the world (Douglas 1982; Asad 1999, 2003; Berger 1997, 1998, 1999; Quarles van Ufford and Schoffeleers 1988; Comaroff 1994; Van der Veer 1996, 1999; Reidhead 1998; Turner 1997; Glazier 2000; Wuthnow 1996; Firth 1981; Bax 1985). Asad writes, "The secularization thesis seems less and less plausible . . . because what many would anachronistically call religion was always involved in the world of power . . . The categories of politics and religion turn out to implicate each other more profoundly than we thought" (Asad 1999, 192). The myth that religion has become irrelevant dies hard—especially among university faculty who consider themselves too enlightened to be bothered with religion. The essays in *The Desecularization of the World* demonstrate that religion has not only survived in the modern world, it is flourishing (Berger 1999).

Further, many anthropologists "have viewed religion as an illusion (science gone wrong)" (Poewe 1994, 236). In an article by Edith Turner describing "Religion and Culture in Present-day anthropology" she writes, "There are certain implicit anthropological tenets to studying religion: religion is a cultural construct and therefore unconscious deception; Western intellectuals cannot "believe" in religion" (Turner 1997, 38). "When we speak of the primitive world it is permissible in any civilized company to refer to supernaturalism. With reference to our own society, however, it often is regarded as a mark of militant atheism" (Norbeck 1961). Evans-Pritchard writes accusingly, "Social anthropology has been the product of minds which, with very few exceptions, regarded all religion as outmoded superstition, suited no doubt to a pre-scientific age and historically justified, like classes in the eyes of Marxists, for a given period, but now useless, and even without ethical value, and worse than useless because it stood in the way of a rational regeneration of mankind and social progress" (1972, 205). Animosity towards Christianity seems particularly rampant among anthropologists. One anthropologist writes, "My freedom from the things that nearly destroyed me (and that continue to haunt me) would come from studying them, and wrestling with them in order to expose their secret. At that point, just short of stomping on them and destroying them, for some reason my private battle stops. Today, I have no love for the Southern Baptists, but I can almost say 'Billy Graham' without sneering" (Richardson 1975, 17; Stipe 1980).

Harding, an anthropologist studying Christian fundamentalists in America, encountered many difficulties within the anthropology community because of the choice of her subject (1987, 1988, 1991, 2000). She places fundamentalists in the same marginalized space as homosexuals and women asking why academic studies have marginalized the study of Christianity "at our meetings, in our publications, and our funding" (1991, 392). "Implicitly, I am arguing along the way that many modernist presuppositions still operate uncritically within contemporary studies of politics and culture, thwarting scrupulous interpretation and re-representation of some cultural 'others,' specifically those deemed inappropriately religious or otherwise problematic or repugnant, and generating a radically parochial imaginary of the margins in which only sanctioned cultural 'others' survive" (Harding 1991, 376). Wagner shares that because of her choice to study "conservative Christian schools" she was confronted with the issue of loyalty from both her colleagues as well as her informants (Wagner 1997, 94). She cites a 1991 study that revealed 65 percent of anthropologists polled claimed no religion. "In this national survey of college faculty, anthropologists had the highest percentage of nonbelievers" (1997, 95). "The loyalty issues related to studying Christianity are unique to the study of religion. When studying an exotic religion in another culture, the ethnographer is not questioned about loyalty . . . If, for example, researchers are admitted believers, their ethnographic work will be dismissed with, 'They're too faith-committed' . . . If they are successful in convincing the interlocutors that they are not believers, the ethnographers will be criticized for not being able to experience what believers do" (1997, 95–96). Christianity as a subject presents a number of problems for the anthropology community. Pandian suggests these problems exist because both groups are competing for answers to similar questions about the nature of humanity and the world (1991, 195). Poewe, an anthropologist studying "charismatic Christianity as a global culture," found that the "experience of Pentecostal churches confronts us with our narrowness: the narrowness of the scholar who must despiritualize religion to conform with colleagues' expectations of conducting a scientific work; the narrowness of the theologian who is unwilling to accommodate his exegesis to the oral narrative style of the majority in his church; the narrowness of the missionary and lay Christian who is afraid to learn something about the Gospel that is in contradiction to what he thought the Gospel was" (Poewe 1994, 21).

POWER AND IDEATION WITHIN RELIGION

Anthropologists should approach religions and their ritual practices as disciplines taught and learned, as well as created and experienced, in conditions imposed by power.

—Talal Asad, *Anthropological Conceptions of Religion*

Geertz concluded that "no theoretical advances of major importance" have been made in the anthropology of religion since the Second World War and that it "is in fact in a state of general stagnation" (Geertz 1973, 87). Geertz played a significant role in advancing the anthropological study of religion by claiming that religion should be understood first as part of a cultural system of symbols and meanings (1973, 90). His interpretive approach is widely used not only by anthropologists of religion but also by practitioners in the field of missiology and theology. But Geertz does not help us with understanding how a particular community's system of meaning is embedded within a larger political, economic, and theological system whose significance can only be understood by examining the historical and social processes of change that shaped and legitimized such a system (Asad 1983). Bax, writing in 1993, states that Geertz's claim of theoretical stagnation within the anthropology of religion remains relevant due in part to the continued culturalist approach and bias (Bax 1993; Wax 1984).

This criticism of Geertz may not be completely fair today, as Geertz seems to be evolving by recently acknowledging the importance of locating power and conflict within the interpretive process of meaning making (Geertz 2000, 167–86). "In the real world, 'meaning,' 'identity,' 'power,' and 'experience' are hopelessly entangled, mutually implicative, and 'religion' can no more be founded upon or reduced to the last, that is, 'experience,' than it can to any of the others" (2000, 184). He criticizes his own former work describing his first field work experience when he was sent off " to locate bits of Javanese culture deemed religious, marking them off from other bits called, no more helpfully, secular, and subjecting the whole to functional analysis" (2000, 15).

There are encouraging signs then, that this stagnation is coming to an end with recent research trends that add the domain of power to the study of religion (Asad 1983; Bax 1985, 1987, 1991; Wolf 1984, 1991, 1999; Ong 1988, 1990; van der Veer 1996, 1999; Comaroffs 1985, 1986, 1991, 1993; Bourdillon 1995; Buckland 1995; Bourdieu

1993; Yanagisako 1995; Bowie 1998; Cunningham 1995; Dube 1998; Schoffeleers 1985; Stirrat 1992; Apter 1992; Sahlins 1981, 1985; Bloch 1989; Firth 1981; Kertzer 1988; Lambek 2000; Ortner 1989; Shaw 1995). Research on religion usually focuses either on material conditions or on symbolic meaning. "It stems ultimately from oppositions (between matter and mind, the concrete and the concept, and so on) at the ontological roots of our social thought—oppositions which persist despite growing agreement that the primary processes involved in the production of the everyday world are inseparably material and meaningful" (Comaroff and Comaroff 1991, 8).

Asad criticized Geertz for missing the crucial interconnections of power and religion " not merely in the sense in which political interests have used religion to justify a given social order or to challenge and change it (an important question in itself) but in the sense in which power constructs religious ideology, establishes the preconditions for distinctive kinds of religious personality, authorizes specifiable religious practices and utterances, produces religiously defined knowledge" (Asad 1983, 237). Building upon Asad, Mart Bax continued the criticism within anthropology that "it has been almost standard practice to treat religion and politics as the private reserves of separate sub-disciplines that almost invariably become mired in their own theoretical perspectives (Bax 1987, 1). His monumental paper shows how "religious regimes play an important role in processes of state-formation and state-development" and vice versa how "for their expansion, religious regimes are often dependent upon states" (Bax 1987, 3). These religious regimes are "power constellations" that can only be understood properly by a "focus on the external conditions and the immanent forces that generate a particular attitude toward power" (Bax 1987, 9). "For him . . . Christianity is a dynamic and ever-evolving power constellation whose diverse parts or 'regimes' struggle against each other as often as they converge. The stereotypical dichotomy of heresy and orthodoxy overlooks the extent of internal competition" (Schneider and Lindenbaum 1987, 2). Although this research perspective draws from earlier Marxist theories of religion, it also makes a break from this tradition. As Firth notes, "Religion is by no means always a simple reflection of current relations of production or a historical expression of earlier material conditions . . . A rigorous economic determinism is insufficient explanation" for two important reasons. First, "Religion can be used for political challenge, revolutionary alternative and resistance" and second, "Religion does not appear to wither away given Marx's material conditions in a socialist country" (Firth 1981, 593).

Eric Wolf supports Bax's research directive emphasizing that "religion also generates vectors (of power), at once economic, political, and sanctifying" (Schneider and Rapp 1995, 4; Wolf 1984, 1991). Wolf interprets Bax's call for a research perspective as one that "rather than treating religion purely as a realm of meaning, without reference to issues of power, or dealing with politics as the province of power, without raising questions of meaning . . . suggests that research study power and meaning in their 'antagonistic interdependencies'" (Wolf 1991, 1). As Lambek notes, it is important to see religions as both "embodied and imagined worlds" (Lambek 2000, 311). Wolf's concept of structural power operative over the political economy is central to this study of Christianity in Hong Kong "precisely because it allows us to delineate how the forces of the world impinge upon the people we study" (Wolf 1990, 587). This study follows Wolf in terms of finding "ways of interrogating such materials (case studies) to define the relations of power that are played out in social arrangements and cultural configurations, and to trace out the possible ways in which these relations of power implicate ideas" (Wolf 1999).

THEOLOGY AS A SOCIAL DOMAIN

The world of humankind constitutes a manifold, a totality of interconnected processes, and inquiries that disassemble this totality into bits and then fail to reassemble it falsify reality. Concepts like "nation," and "society," and "culture" (and theology) name bits and threaten to turn names into things.

— Eric Wolf, *Europe and the People Without History*

It will be important to define the social domain this research studies but not in such a way as to artificially remove and separate theology by definition from other domains. This study rejects any rigid definitions that reify and universalize theology as a social domain along with recent criticisms of definitions of religion (Buckland 1995; Bowie 1998; Geertz 2000; Bax 1987, 1993; Asad 1983, 1993, 1999, 2003; Bowie 2000; El-Zein 1977; Lambek 2000; Ortner 1978; Stirrat 1992; Van der Veer 1999; Wax 1984; Shaw 1995; Saler 1993, 2002; Wolf 1999). Although universal definitions of religion (like culture) are problematic, I think it is worthwhile to keep the concept.

Feminist anthropology helps in this study by challenging universal concepts of theology that remove issues of power that exclude and marginalize others (Shaw 1995; Bowie 1998, 2000, 2003; Yanagisako 1995). Kwok Pui-lan, someone doing theology as a Chinese woman, has pointed to the relationship between power and theological truth using Michel Foucault's concept of the political economy of truth. There is a reciprocal relationship between truth and power. Theology is "never simply a religious matter," but a matter "imbued with the issues of authority and power" (Kwok 1995, 300). That it is to say, there are "power mechanisms which govern the production and repression of truth," (Kwok 1995, 300) as well as "ensures its survival under the mask of knowledge" (Foucault 1980, 141-142). "The idea that knowledge never functions outside power seems theologically very significant" (Volf et al. 1996, 108). The exercise of structural power depends upon control and production of culturally available knowledge. "Language and discourse are among the ultimate means of production" (Verdery 1991, 420). "Power is thus never external to signification—it inhabits meaning and is its champion in stabilization and defense" (Wolf 2001, 396). Theology then is inevitably mired in issues of power that brings theology into relationship with other social domains. This research studies how power is involved in the creation and maintenance of local theological truths.

Feminist anthropology also helps us see that theology is as much about gender, class, and ethnicity as about God. Theological domains are not as discrete as they are articulated. Evans-Pritchard argued that what Durkheim "calls sacred and profane are on the same level of experience, and far from being cut off from one another, they are so closely intermingled as to be inseparable ... I have never found the dichotomy was of much use" (1965, 65). I would agree, "The confinement of cultural exegesis to the space inside domains is especially rigid when it comes to the sacred. Sacred meanings may be read into other domains, but the reverse is not acceptable. Indeed, what defines the sacred is that which is sealed off from readings emanating from other cultural domains. The meaning of the sacred can only be revealed by those with cultural authority to interpret it. If the sacred is open to divergent readings by people who bring with them ideas associated with human social life, the claim that it is 'god-given' is undermined" (Yanagisako and Delaney 1995, 12–13).

"Reading across religious domains is, therefore, inevitably both subversive and threatening to the status quo, at least within religious systems that are hierarchically structured and in which access to religious power is in the hands of ritual specialists" (Bowie 1998, 53). Reading theology across social domains then often amounts to a charge of "sacrilege" or what one feminist theologian calls "indecent theology" (Althaus-Reid 2000). This research exposes the profane in what is often disguised as the sacred in an attempt to understand how theology is embedded in relations of power.

This research takes as its subject ideas about God and the embodiment of those ideas in practice. It is not about a metaphysical search for God. It is a grounded anthropological inquiry into ideas (theologies) about God. "What makes a discussion theological is not its subject matter (theology can talk about any and everything) but its manner of treatment, its reference of all things to God" (Boff 1987). For this study, theology does not refer to the predominantly western notion of a static formal systematic study of the nature of God. Rather, it refers to the dynamic informal discourses and practices that local people, not just professionals, use to situate themselves in relation to God, to other people, and to their environment. Theology is space of signifying practice, where human agents construct and negotiate meanings, and further by implication, society and history. "But theology ... is much more than a worldview. It represents a concerted effort to understand, question, interpret, challenge and/or engage the world" (Glazier 2000, 411). Theology is not merely an interpretive experience because it seeks to engage the world by affecting change. The specification of theologies in cultural terms can only be part of our task. "We must also know how these cultural forms engage with the material resources and organizational arrangements of the world they try to affect or transform" (Wolf 1999, 280). Theologies are both envisioned and embodied.

The concept of theology this research uses also benefits from insights from practice theory (Ortner, Bourdieu, Ong, Comaroffs, and Cunningham). The research finds it useful to locate theology within discourse as well as within practice. Theology happens as the mediation between two important moments, the objective (structuration) and the subjective (agency). This research finds it useful to study theology as practice embedded within a political economy and context of power (Ong 1999, 5). This understanding of theology encompasses struggles over human practice, meaning, and representation in relation to the changing political-economic context.

This study explores theology as a constellation of contradictory and contesting processes. It is a site for meaning making albeit meaning that is severely constrained and shaped by historical and material conditions and power wielding. Theology will always be contextual. Any notion of an authentic universal theology as an autonomous reality no longer seems possible, except as ecclesiastical hegemony or naïve fiction. Theologies, as discourse on all things in relation to God, legitimize as well as challenge a particular set of social relations. It is this dimension of power and its relation to theological ideas that this research is particularly interested in examining. Finally, this study defines theologians as those who study and purport to understand and promulgate the meaning of religion. For this research, "Anthropologists must go further than the theologians. Apart from explicating the meaning of texts, we need to explore causal relationships between patterns of behavior" (Bourdillon 1995, 51).

RESEARCH DESIGN AND METHODOLOGY

As an anthropologist, I believe that theoretical discussions need to be grounded in cases, in observed streams of behavior, and in recorded texts. I want to find ways of interrogating such materials to define the relations of power that are played out in social arrangements and cultural configurations, and to trace out the possible ways in which these relations of power implicate ideas.

—Eric Wolf, *Envisioning Power*

This qualitative research project utilized multiple ethnographic research methods including: participant observation in key settings, informal and semi-structured interviews, focus groups, informal socializing, archival work, and general reading of newspapers and documents produced by the groups I studied. This project utilized research from existing data (surveys, articles, books, sermons, music) located at local seminaries, universities, and research institutions. This methodological triangulation will increase the potential validity of the data.

Over a period of almost two years between August 1999 and June 2001, I conducted seventy-six formal interviews with primarily church and parachurch leadership. I selected subjects for the research study using purposive sampling because of limited resources and for a concern to include a representative sample of theological and denominational communities. The annual *Hong Kong Church Directory* published by the Chinese Christian Literature Council provided a useful resource for purposive sampling. Although this selection method produces a bias, its benefits of establishing rapport and trust with the research participants will outweigh its costs of a non-probability sample (Bernard 1995; Pelto and Pelto 1978). Although non-probability sampling methods reduce the potential external validity, research shows that "when backed by ethnographic data, studies based on these sampling techniques (purposive) are often highly credible" (Bernard 1995, 94). In addition to a purposive sample, the research used snowball sampling as a way of discovering and understanding social networks (Bernard 1995, 97). This snowball sampling technique began with previous research conducted under a NSF pre-dissertation ethnographic field research grant of the 1997 Hong Kong handover events.

The initial phase of the research process began with reestablishing contact with previous key informants and organizations studied during preliminary research in 1997. Participant observation and informal interviews began immediately in the social setting of churches, homes, and parachurch offices and included events such as worship, Bible study, business meetings, social gatherings, celebrations, and conferences. I attended church services of over twenty different denominational groups. On a monthly basis, I attended the Hong Kong Ministerium meeting where a guest speaker led in a discussion of an issue relevant to the Christian community of Hong Kong. I attended numerous other Christian conferences regularly including the important "Mission Consultation of the Hong Kong Churches in the 21st Century," organized by the Hong Kong Christian Council.

Six months into my fieldwork experience I received a phone call from the director of Lay Theological Education Division at a local seminary. "Will you teach a course called *Communication Models and Cross-cultural Mission?*" she asked. The proposition caught me off guard. I came to the field to learn, not to teach. The idea of "teaching" a seminary course and thus becoming an active theological participant with my study group did not seem to fit my idea of participant observation and data gathering. I would later discover that this three-hour weekly classroom experience provided an excellent learning environment and a regular focus group for my research. The classroom became a rich and intimate context to confront my own presuppositions, make clear my own commitments, ask questions and discover new ones, explore ideas, develop relationships, and receive ongoing feedback on my research. Believing that good teaching begins with finding the right questions rather than finding the right answers, we developed together a learning community where we became co-learners.

I collected and examined surveys and research by and of the local Christian communities from local research centers including the Hong Kong Church Renewal Movement, the Hong Kong Christian Institute, the Hong Kong Christian Council, the Christian Study Centre on Chinese Religion and Culture, Chung Chi College, and Hong Kong Baptist University among many others. The research produced a very extensive bibliography of Christianity in Hong Kong. Another useful source of survey data came from dissertation research (DMin and DMiss) produced by local pastors before the 1997 handover. Many local pastors went to the United States for applied doctoral research to study how to handle the impending "crisis." The researcher did coding and content analysis of local Christian journals and newspapers such as the *CGST Journal, Jian Dao, Christian Times, Christian Weekly, Ching Feng, Tripod, HKCC News and Views,* the *HKCI Newsletter,* and many other smaller publications. Archival research provided an important source of data for this research project.

In addition to participant observation within the Christian community, I was regularly involved with the local academic and research communities located at the Chinese University of Hong Kong (University Service Center, Anthropology Department, Religion and Theology Department), Hong Kong University (Centre of Asian Studies and Hong Kong Cultural Studies Program), Hong Kong University of Science and Technology, and the South East Asian Research Center. I became an active member of the Hong Kong Anthropology Society and the Hong Kong Royal Asiatic Society providing connections with local and visiting researchers including Aihwa Ong, Helen Siu, David Faure, Alan Smart, Paul Cohen, Andrew Walder, Mark Selden, Deborah Davis, David Zweig, and Immanuel Wallerstein. In addition to regular lectures and an anthropology film festival, I participated in regular group outings to visit research sites of interest. We participated in the *tai-ping hung-chiu* ceremony (New Year's festivities) in Fanling Wai and the rededication ceremonies of the Hung Sing temple at the fishing village of Kau Sai Chau where Barbara Ward conducted much of her anthropological research beginning in the 1950s. Of particular interest to this research was a visit to former Bethanie Church of the Missions Etrangeres de Paris (French Catholic Mission established between 1873–1875) that included personal reflections by Father Peter, a local Chinese priest born and raised at this mission.

This research borrows from Burawoy's research method called the "extended case study method" (1991). Before the project began, I intended to utilize grounded theory, but later decided the idea of collecting and analyzing data sui generis was unrealistic. The research project emerged then out of a desire to build upon the existing theoretical work of Eric Wolf, particularly *Envisioning Power* (1999), through an additional case study. Burawoy is helpful here. For Burawoy, analysis is viewed as "a continual process, mediating between field data and existing theory" (Burawoy 1991, 11). There is an ongoing "dialogue between theory and data whose goal is explanation" (1991, 5). The research methods evolved as I processed the field data in light of Eric Wolf's theoretical attempt to explicate the relationships between power and ideas. As the ethnographic data were collected, the significant and culturally relevant issues and questions were identified to explore in greater depth during focus group and key informant interviews.

This research method necessitated keeping three kinds of field notes: notes on methods and techniques, descriptive or ethnographic notes, and analytic notes (Bernard 1995, 186). I maintained ethnographic notes in a file labeled "field notes" and methodological and analytic notes in a separate file labeled "dissertation journal." Another important source for notes made during field research was personal notes on the relationship of the researcher to the research, noting such things as bias, emotional health, and frustrations. These notes were maintained in the "dissertation journal." I intended to use NUD*IST, a qualitative research software program, to process and analyze the interviews and field notes, but in the end utilized NUD*IST's methods and procedures using Microsoft Word and coding by hand. One reason for opting to use Word is that I did not have the large amounts of transcribed interview materials I intended. I found reluctance on the part of many informants to allow tape recordings of our conversations because of the sensitive nature of the questions and shared information. By taking notes during the interviews, I gained more valuable information than if I used a tape recorder. I decided that this gain outweighed the cost of fewer quotes and possibly a loss of information. I attempted to write-up the interview in "field notes" as soon as possible on the day of the interview utilizing written notes and quotes to get the best possible transcription of the interview.

This research project encountered a number of problems related to research design, methods, and data collection. These problems were in part related to the nature of the research topic, the research site, and the "elite" research subject. I encountered problems from the start because I was "studying up" within the fast-paced life of a global cityscape (Nader 1969). Many executives did not have time for a student learner of their culture. After a meeting with visiting lecturer and anthropologist Fred Blake, I decided to alter my role to expert by dressing in a suit, carrying a briefcase, using a cell phone, and handing out name cards. It made a great difference. After this change of appearance, I was amazed how much more time and information informants were willing to share with me. The people I studied were highly educated professionals with very busy schedules. During one informal interview I was asked to explain the missiological perspective behind the research. I explained that I was interested in exploring the relationship between culture and Christianity in Hong Kong but was shortly interrupted with the direct question, "Why here in Hong Kong?" They went on to express their opinion that "culture" in Hong Kong was irrelevant to missiological concerns of Christianity in Hong Kong because they were "modernized" just like the United States and Europe. This research disagrees that the study of "culture" is irrelevant. Nevertheless, this informant does raise an important issue this research struggles with regarding the nature of "culture" and "Christianity" when "they" look so much like "us."

A further limitation and difficulty faced by this research was the nature of the research questions themselves. While the subject of politics or economics by themselves was not taboo, the relationship of faith to political and economic practices was considered a sensitive if not taboo topic for discussion. This kind of data collection often required that trust was established first, and quite frankly this was not always possible. The researchers at the Hong Kong Church Renewal Movement shared the same frustrations I encountered. Church leaders in particular were hesitant to share what they viewed as private information and potentially threatening. More needs to be done on the anthropology of the private, the unseen, and the "immoral" despite the difficulties.

Because the research subjects spoke English better than the researcher could have learned Cantonese in a short time, all interviews except two were conducted using English. I used a translator for the other two interviews. A few meetings began with the use of conversational Mandarin, but the interviews always moved into English because of my limited Chinese speaking ability. The research was multi-sited requiring a change in methods and focus that included more of a social networks' framework. The research moved away from the description of the everyday life of the average Hong Kong Christian. The theoretical interest of the research moved the research focus to macro-level concerns and a particular group of elite and marginal Christian leaders. The research runs the risk of being criticized (as Ortner has done of Wolf) for missing the ethnographic or the practice of real people. I wish more consideration of this problem had been dealt with in the research design. Better design and methods could have been used in order to hold in tension the perspectives of practice and structure. This research focused on descriptions of structural processes at the expense of descriptions of everyday practices.

Hong Kong as a "virtual state" and global city provided its own difficulties as a research site in an urban modern environment. Participation observation in global city such as Hong Kong also included visits with friends and research subjects to operas, plays, concerts, dinners, dancing, karaoke, shopping malls, and art museums. It was impossible to distinguish the local from the global in Hong Kong. The Hong Kong experience frustrates any attempt to define "culture" in any static sense. Discussions with informants could easily include discussions of world politics and economics as they influenced Hong Kong life. The informants were knowledgeable of stock markets, wines, cigars, European automobiles, and Paris fashion trends because these are what they consumed.

Rosaldo warns that when studying people like "us", anthropologists usually find no "culture," just "empty space" and "cultural invisibility" (Rosaldo 1988, 1989). This is because of wrong assumptions and wrong ideas about what 'culture' really is. I think the problem of social location was exacerbated because the subject was Christianity in a modern metropolis. The people I studied looked very similar to people back home. Rosaldo says it is common to find a "cultural blank slate" (from our perspective) where there is greater social mobility, advanced capitalism, and/or a nation-state achieving full citizenship. He suggests we turn our attention to the border zones or boundaries within the society and the articulation and practice of differences. I found this method useful for getting at issues relevant to power and difference related to theoretical commitments of this research project. The participant observation shortly moved away from study of the local church congregation to a study of parachurch organizations at the margins of Christianity as well as Hong Kong society. It would be wrong to generalize concerning the experience of every Hong Kong Christian or community from the ethnographic data collected. The research focused on the social networks and relations among the leaders of the Christian community. The research focused on the contested struggle over the meaning and practice of Christianity among Christian leadership. In doing so, the research discovered that the struggle was more often less about the meaning of Christianity as about institutional survival and organizational power.

CRITICAL MISSIOLOGICAL ANTHROPOLOGY: EPISTEMOLOGY, ASSUMPTIONS, AND LIMITATIONS

Indeed, research in the field, by which every anthropological career begins, is mother and nurse of doubt, the philosophical attitude par excellence. This "anthropological doubt" does not only consist of knowing that one knows nothing, but of resolutely exposing what one thought one knew—and one's very ignorance—to the buffetings and denials directed at one's most cherished ideas and habits by other ideas and habits best able to rebut them.

—Claude Levi-Strauss

A number of recent writers have argued that cross-cultural theory inevitably involves the author in an arrogant domination of the subject being discussed. This does not seem to me to be true. Rather, it is the self-conscious refusal to engage in attempts at explanation which I feel is the danger for the anthropologist . . . I believe that to propose a theory is to implicate ourselves as much as other peoples in the explanation . . . it is only by attempting to understand in this way that we can move on, even if the conclusions reached are provisional and incomplete. It is surely by this essay into understanding that we acknowledge our connectedness with and involvement in the world, and the continuity between our own and other societies.

—Maurice Bloch

This research seeks explanation of causal relationships rather than just description or interpretation as is consistent with the perspective of Eric Wolf. The epistemological perspective is that of a critical realist that rejects the extremes of positivism and self-reflexive subjectivism. The perspective is critical because it remains "professionally suspicious of our categories and models ... we can understand the quest for explanation as approximations of truth rather than as truth itself" (Wolf 2001, 386).

Further, there is a commitment within this research project to seek explanations in order to engage the world's problems. There exists the intention to apply the research. This research follows in the footsteps of Eric Wolf as well as Roy Rappaport. Like other political-economic studies, this research project utilizes a theoretical framework that seeks to address policy relevant issues. The research focuses on the issues related to the generation, control, and use of theological knowledge that validates and prioritizes a capitalist modern understanding of the world that in turn often marginalizes alternative viewpoints and practices. "Those of us who are interested in the significance of religion in our own societies cannot ignore how it relates to other social institutions. We are interested in how religion relates to differences in wealth and class in society; how it relates to technological changes in such things as health and agriculture; how it relates to education . . . In the face of the AIDS epidemic, it is useful to know how and in what circumstances religion might affect sexual practices" (Bourdillon 1993, 228). The World Bank and IMF have recently acknowledged the importance of religion and faith to the development process by creating the World Faiths Development Dialogue council in 2001.

The primary research question asks how theologies are embedded in particular socio-cultural and political-economic contexts in terms of structural power. A corollary to that question is to ask more specifically how theologies, which are taken to be embedded in social and political-economic processes, are connected to the health and wholeness of humanity (particularly in material ways), and then how compromised human well-being further threatens the social fabric. This last question comes from the work of Goodman and Leatherman's collection *Building a New Biocultural Synthesis* (1998). This research seeks to use anthropological perspectives and methods to connect theological discourses and practices to the reality of the poor and powerless. In the same way that one group of anthropologists examine culture alongside biology in order to better understand and better practice the "mission" for a healthier humanity, I am working to connect culture, power and theology in order to build a healthier humanity. They provide a critical medical anthropology in order to judge the medical enterprise that is supposed to serve human health. I am working to provide a critical missiological anthropology that engages in criticism of the theological and Christian mission enterprise that is to suppose to restore humanity's wholeness. This research intends to move toward an engaged missiological anthropology or critical theological anthropology.

I agree with Scheper-Hughes who says, "If I did not believe that ethnography could be used as a tool for critical reflection and as a tool for human liberation, what kind of perverse cynicism would keep me returning again and again to disturb the waters of Bom Jesus da Mata?" (Scheper-Hughes 1992, 28). In a recent *Anthropology Newsletter* (1998), Reidhead and Reidhead raise an important challenge to the anthropological community that this research project seeks to meet. "For anthropologists it is ethical to engage most all of the institutions of society, from education to marketing, in basic and applied research. We seem to have an informal prohibition, however, against an applied anthropology of religion, though there are some exceptions" (Reidhead and Reidhead 1998, 36). They offer three challenges to an expanded vision of the anthropology of religion and its relevance: (1) health disciplines' research and use of religious knowledge and practice; (2) religious decision makers who use anthropology; and (3) subjects who have diverse understandings. They share their own experiences of problems and successes when collaborating with religious subjects. They suggest it is not only possible but also relevant for anthropology to become engaged in religious discourse anthropology although grounded in ethnographic research.

This research perspective leads then to value commitments and criticisms but does so with epistemological humility and acknowledgement of limitations. "The issue is not whether we can make judgments about other cultures; the problem is how to make such judgments and how to remain aware of our limitations inherent in them" (Bourdillon 1995, 51). This perspective arises out of this research's understanding of culture and theology shared by Bourdillon. "Culture is not something shared by all members of a society... It is rather a mass of ideas and behavior within which individuals in different ways struggle for power, or wealth, and often for other values. I wish to take part in the struggle for other values" (Bourdillon 1995, 53). I hope this dissertation contributes to this struggle for other values over the struggle for power.

3

Descriptive Integration

THIS DESCRIPTIVE INTEGRATION, AS Eric Wolf calls it, locates the research in space and time, describes the relevant structural relations across social domains, and defines the external forces that shape the experiences of Hong Kong people. The research studies Hong Kong during a period of perceived crisis or "high drama" (Wolf 1999, 17). While Wolf admits the "distinctions between periods of normality and periods of crisis is to a large extent fictitious," he continues that case studies of perceived crisis may help "magnify and display structure and themes that might remain more muted and veiled" (Wolf 1999, 17). While the research agenda focuses on how Hong Kong Christians responded ideologically to the purported crisis, it is important to begin with an understanding of the historical trajectory that accounts for Hong Kong society's perspective of the 1997 event as a crisis.

STRUCTURAL ORGANIZATION OF CHRISTIANITY IN HONG KONG

Perhaps as a tourist visiting Hong Kong it would be difficult to see the influence of Christianity on social structures and relations.[1] Stop and ask Hong Kong people to identify their religion, and you will find the majority claim no religion. The *South China Morning Post* reported in 1999 that 64 percent of respondents in Hong Kong claim no religion whereas only

---

1. The Hong Kong Chinese use the word "Christianity," "*jidu jiao*," (Mandarin) "*geidukgaau*," (Cantonese) to refer specifically to Protestantism as opposed to Catholicism, "*tianzhu jiao*," or "*tinjyugaau*." See note in Madsen (1998:165n.23). For a dictionary definition of these words see Kwan Choi Wah, The Right Word in Cantonese (1996). This research focuses on the Protestant dimensions of the Christian scene and therefore my use of "Christianity" most often refers to Protestantism except when noted.

about 10 percent of the population identify themselves as Christians.[2] But stop and ask Hong Kong people their opinion of Christianity and you will find the majority view it favorably as an important contributor to the development of Hong Kong's prosperity and stability. "When asked where they want to send their children to school, invariably the answer is *Jiaohui Xuexiao* (school run by the church)" (Kwok 1994, 85). Although Christians represent a minority group, on the other hand, they embody and legitimize a majority ethos. "The influence of the churches is far out of proportion to the membership" (Luk 1990, 570). Richard Madsen describes the role of the Catholic Church in Hong Kong as a "moral force within Hong Kong's civil society" (1998, 142–143).

Christian organizations exert a great deal of influence on Hong Kong society. Altogether Christian organizations operate sixty percent of Hong Kong's social services, forty percent of the primary and secondary schools, and twenty percent of the hospitals and clinics. The institutional church controls the second largest source of labor employing more than one hundred thousand workers. Protestant organizations alone operate over twenty seminaries, 183 evangelistic parachurch groups, forty-five mission organizations, fifty-seven bookstores, two weekly newspapers, twenty-five campgrounds, 624 social service units, ten hospitals, thirty clinics and other medical services, 273 kindergartens, 192 primary schools, 144 secondary schools, and three universities (HKCRM 2000). A building or a second floor flat visibly bares witness to a Christian presence in every Hong Kong neighborhood with over 1,212 Protestant congregations[3] and more than one hundred Roman Catholic parishes.[4] The majority of those serving in government were educated through

---

2. About 250 thousand people belong to the Roman Catholic Church. One hundred thousand belong to mainline Protestant churches and another 245 thousand belong to a variety of evangelical Protestant churches (see HKCRM survey 1999). The 1999 survey shows little difference from an earlier survey conducted by May M. Cheng and Wong Siu-lun of the Chinese University of Hong Kong: No religion 60.2 percent; Folk religion 15.3 percent; Buddhist 11.6 percent; Catholic 4.5 percent; Protestant 8.4 percent (Cheng and Wong 1997). Also, see earlier surveys by Harry C. Hui (1991); Berkowitz et al. (1969); Robert Mitchell (1974); John T. Myers (1981); Lang and Ragvald (1993); and Chan Shun-hing (1995, 44–65).

3. Ratio of the number of churches to the overall population—1:7986 (1980); 1:6521 (1989); 1:5715 (1994); 1:6061 (HKCRM 1999).

4. August 1996 statistics are from the Hong Kong Catholic Church Directory report: 243,000 Catholics (4 percent of population), 326 priests, 559 female religious, 329 schools, 103 socio-medical institutions (Leung 1998).

one of the elite Christian schools and many of them are active church members. A 1996 survey showed self-identified Christians occupied 22.5 percent of all positions in government agencies (Xue 1996). Martin Lee, chairman of the Democratic Party, "explicitly credits his Catholic education with giving him his sense of social responsibility" (Madsen 1998, 13; Kwong 2000, 54–55; Smith 1985).

The 1,212 Protestant congregations, organized by sixty denominations, as well as by more than two hundred independent church groups, have no common organizational umbrella. The largest denominations include Baptists, Christian Missionary & Alliance, Lutherans, Church of Christ in China, Anglicans, Peace Evangelical, Assemblies of God, and Methodists. The Baptist Convention of Hong Kong, largest of all the denominations, manages 114 churches (Li and Lee 1996). Attempts were made to create more unity among churches as 1997 approached, but a spirit of competition and disunity prevails as most groups focus on self-preservation and church growth.

The number of parachurch organizations has steadily increased since the early 1970s. Parachurch organizations exist as extensions of the church which remain structurally separate from any denomination or local church decision-making body. They work alongside churches usually focused on a single agenda that the churches are unable or unwillingly to do. Most engage in specialized evangelistic work by targeting a specific group defined for example by age, ethnicity, class, or social dysfunction. Hong Kong parachurch groups have focused heavily on youth and college students. Other parachurch organizations work in the areas of communication and media. A number of groups organized to focus on issues related to the 1997 issue. My research examines in particular a smaller number of parachurch groups, active in social justice, advocacy, and development, which criticize the local church for neglecting roles of the church that they have now assumed.[5] These parachurch groups focus on the needs of the poor and disenfranchised within the local political-economy.

---

5. Examples include: Hong Kong Christian Institute (HKCI); Hong Kong Christian Industrial Committee (CIC); Industrial Evangelical Fellowship (IEF); Hong Kong Women Christian Council (HKWCC); Christian Sentinels; Christians for Hong Kong Society; Justice and Peace Commission for the Roman Catholic Church; Jubilee Ministries; Mission to New Arrivals; and Society for Truth and Light.

There are also a number of important parachurch organizations that exist to facilitate cooperative Christian activities and to further connect Hong Kong churches into a larger regional and international network of Christians. The oldest group, the Hong Kong Chinese Christian Church Union (HKCCCU), founded in 1915, includes a membership of 293 local Chinese churches. This group primarily manages Hong Kong's two Christian cemeteries, organizes the large evangelistic crusades, and publishes the Christian Weekly. They control a great deal of capital but have been largely unsuccessful at building a strong network of cooperation. The Hong Kong Christian Council (HKCC), founded in 1954, has traditionally functioned as the international spokesperson for Hong Kong churches although the membership represents mostly mainline denominations and congregations. It was initially formed to coordinate churches' social services to the surge of mainland Chinese immigrants. Today, the HKCC also represents a powerful network of churches that play an important role in the development of the local political-economy and networking local churches with China and the international community. The Chinese Coordination Center for World Evangelism (CCCOWE), founded in 1976, represents a strong network internationally for coordinating efforts to evangelize Chinese communities throughout the world and in China. The Hong Kong Church Renewal Movement (HKCRM), founded in 1983, considers itself to be the evangelical equivalent to the HKCC. They emerged shortly after Sino-British negotiations began to help renew churches and pastors through research, seminars and counseling and to facilitate the transition of churches through 1997. They have conducted important large-scale quantitative research on Hong Kong churches for their local use. The HKCRM also took over the work of the Hong Kong Evangelism 2000 organization during a merge in 1994 that included the goal of increasing the number of churches in Hong Kong to 2000 by the end of the millennium.

DEMOGRAPHY OF CHRISTIANITY IN HONG KONG

Hong Kong Christians overall could be characterized as young, highly educated, and middle class[6] in outlook (HKCRM 1999).[7] The median age

---

6. The HKCRM's first public reporting of its latest statistics (Dec. 3, 1999) lists the following as "strengths" of the church: "middle class, many professionals, well-educated, flexible and creative, aggressive in evangelism and missions." For similar descriptions, also see Kuang 2003; Liu 1996a; Liu 1996b and Madsen 1998:142.

7. Although this survey is of Protestant Christians, the demography is very similar

of the Hong Kong population is 35.3 years old compared to 31.2 in the Protestant church. Seventy-five percent of Protestant Christians are age forty-four or below. In terms of educational achievement, only 17.5 percent of the general population received tertiary education compared to thirty-three percent of the Christian population. A 1995 survey showed 40.9 percent of those in the general population who had attained a postgraduate level of education were also Christians. Because the level of educational achievement closely relates to socio-economic status, the survey also shows a large number of Christians among the middle and upper class.[8] In terms of vocation, twenty-one percent of Hong Kong's overall population consists of professionals, while the church population is 34 percent professionals. Within the church, these professionals hold the majority of important leadership positions and therefore make the decisions within the church (Liu 1996, 280; Law 1982, 66).

Females make up 60.4 percent of the Protestant population compared to 49.7 percent of the general Hong Kong population. Singles in the general population are more likely to have no religious belief when compared to married persons, but of those singles who believe in a religion 46.2 percent are Protestants (Cheng and Wong 1997, 304). The 1995 survey also showed a significant relationship between place of birth and religious adherence. A high percentage of Christians along with those who claim no religious belief were born within Hong Kong: 68.6 percent of Protestants, 69.9 percent of Catholics, and sixty percent of those claiming no religion (Cheng and Wong 1997, 305).

Only a small number of churches seek to include recent Mainland Chinese immigrants. Li Kin-wah says only ten churches before 1997 focused on including new immigrants as a part of their congregation (Li 1999). The majority of Hong Kong Christians are Chinese like the population. The largest expatriate community is a growing Filipino population of mostly women who largely supply Hong Kong with its

---

to Catholic Christians. For example, see Cheng and Wong's analysis of the CUHK 1995 survey (1997) and Luk's analysis of the CUHK 1988 survey (1990).

8. 58.9 percent of Protestants described themselves as middle or upper-middle class compared to 11.7 percent who described themselves as lower class. 57 percent of Catholics described themselves as middle or upper-middle class. 41.8 percent of those with no religion described themselves as middle or upper-middle class. 44.3 percent of Buddhists described themselves as middle or upper-middle class. 31.7 percent of those participating in folk religion described themselves as middle or upper-middle class (Cheng and Wong 1997, 307–9).

domestic servants. One estimate suggests 120 thousand of the 180 thousand Filipinos are Catholics (Granberg 2000, 18; Ha 1991, 529). A minority of "Westerners" participate in a small number of English speaking churches. The 1999 HKCRM survey notes the use of Cantonese in 1,127 churches, Mandarin in fifty-eight, other Chinese dialects (Hakka and Fujien mostly) in forty-six, English in forty-four, and other foreign languages in six.

Due to the high cost of property and limited availability of land, church congregations find other places to meet rather than build a church building. Hong Kong is known for its second floor churches. Several flats or apartments on the second floor of a commercial or residential building are connected to create a church location. A survey of 1,129 Chinese-speaking churches showed only 147 used their own independent building, 292 used a commercial building, 341 used a residential building, 179 used a school building, and 158 used a social services building. These commercial and residential building spaces are typically rented spaces because of the high cost of property. Those churches that share a building used for social services, schools or study centers during the week are able to do so through cooperation with the government.

The rising property values have also benefited a number of established denominations that already owned a great deal of land and property. As 1997 approached many sold off or traded properties for millions of dollars. There are a smaller number of evangelical churches that have not received land from the government but because of the generosity of wealthy church members are able to purchase second floor flats and a few are even able to buy land to build their own. Because of the space limitations of most church sites, congregations are typically small with 52 percent averaging fewer than one hundred members. Only forty-four have five hundred or more members with the largest church of four thousand and second largest of three thousand.

RELATIONSHIP OF 1997 TO STRUCTURAL ORGANIZATION AND DEMOGRAPHY

When the discussion of the handover really began to seriously be talked about during the foment of the Joint Declaration (1984), those fearful or pessimistic about the future began planning their exit. This exit of Hong Kong citizens since 1984 has not been small and the impact of this "brain drain" has been much greater on the local Christian community than on the population as a whole. For the general Hong Kong population, one in eight persons emigrated or left and returned with a foreign passport since 1989 (Wark 1995, 54; Granberg 2000, 14). Among the Christian population that figure was one in four.

One of the main reasons provided to explain the higher emigration rate among Christians is the social-economic status of its constituency. The church is largely a middle and upper class institution, and therefore they have the means to emigrate (Brown 1993, 246; Coulson 1996, 62–63. With the emigration of so many Hong Kong Christians, a demand was created for the development of Chinese churches in the major cities they emigrated to. A better paying salary as well as a sense of security drew many of Hong Kong's most senior pastors away to popular emigration destinations such as Toronto, Vancouver, Los Angeles, San Francisco, and Sydney. A 1990 seminary graduate reported that half of the eighteen students in his class emigrated to work in Chinese churches in California, Canada and Australia (Wark 1995, 56). According to statistics gathered by the Hong Kong Church Renewal Movement, almost three-fourths of Hong Kong's pastors age thirty to fifty emigrated between 1985 and 1993. Joseph Kuang, a professor at the Chinese University of Hong Kong, said this created a great deal of resentment back in the late 1980s. Many congregations were asking, "if God is calling you away, how come he never calls you to a third world country, but always to California?" As a result of ministerial emigration, the average age of a senior pastor in Hong Kong dropped to age thirty-five by 1995. Luk Fai, director of the Hong Kong Church Renewal Movement (HKCRM), reports that the result of younger and inexperienced leadership has been a high burnout rate among pastors. The HKCRM was originally organized for the primary purpose of counseling pastors and renewing churches. Despite this exit of pastors and local Christians from Hong Kong, statistics from the HKCRM show that the number of churches and the number of people attending churches have grown over this same period.

As 1997 approached, a significant number of people who emigrated in the mid 1980s began to return to Hong Kong with new passports as insurance if things went bad. People returned largely because they found they could not make as much money at their new homes abroad. These returning immigrants created a demand for a new kind of church. International English speaking congregations composed largely of Chinese families are growing up quickly. These returning emigrants report not feeling comfortable in their old traditional churches after experiencing the less traditional megachurch overseas, and they more importantly want a English speaking environment where their young children who have not grown up with Cantonese can feel comfortable.

A number of Cantonese speaking congregations are successfully following their example by creating a consumer friendly church that attracts the upwardly mobile business community, "their fastest-growing demographic according to pastors" (Lee-Young 2000, 4). Worship takes place in skyscrapers, hotels, and community centers along the harbor and in the center of the business district of Hong Kong.

Hong Kong experienced two periods of rapid church growth, one that followed the inauguration of the People's Republic of China in 1949 and another beginning from the Sino-British negotiations in the 1980s until Hong Kong's return to China in 1997. The number of Protestant churches in Hong Kong increased from 634 in 1980 to almost 1,200 in 1999 making 28.9 percent of all Protestant churches less than nine years old while 47.6 percent are over twenty years old (HKCRM 1999). While the overall annual growth of church members increased, the worship attendance growth rate decreased 7.4 percent since 1994. This trend follows the global trend of increasing numbers of Christians but decreasing church attendance. While the HKCRM reports a decrease in overall church attendance, a network of 170 cell churches report an increase of 120 percent over the past five years. This also reflects the global trend of negative growth among denominational churches and positive growth among independent and charismatic churches. The charismatic Christian presence in Hong Kong is small when compared to global trends. Since the early 1980s, the general Protestant reaction to successive charismatic waves has been distrustful and exclusionary (Chan Shun-hing 1995). But as 1997 approached, Christians characterized as charismatic or Pentecostal grew in numbers, especially among the grassroots people of Hong Kong.

The growth of churches and the emigration of ministers up to 1997 created a demand for theological trained workers that continues post 1997. The Hong Kong protestant church employs 2,578 ministers, 56 percent male and 44 percent female. The average age of a minister dropped to age thirty-four (HKCRM 1999). Male ministers predominantly fill the lead ministerial and preaching positions while females take on auxiliary support positions. Although more women than men attend local seminaries, very few of the theologically trained women are ordained clergy. One survey shows only 6 percent of Hong Kong's ordained clergy are women (Coulson 1996, 90). At the same time 54.5 percent of Hong Kong's theological students are women (HKCRM 1999). All of the female ministers I spoke with shared a frustration of their limited access to ministerial roles and limited power in leadership. Where do these theologically trained women work? One seminary class of women all responded they would be seeking work in a parachurch organization or non-ministerial field of work.

Another interesting statistic among ministers is the high mobility or turnover rate: 32 percent serve less than two years in one church, 36 percent work 2–6 years, and 32 percent stay six years or more. Although not reported in a survey, I discovered many of the ministers changing churches were also changing denominations. Denominational leaders often reported that denominational loyalty was low among their ministers. Changing denominations for a higher salary or better position took precedence. This may explain in part the rapid increase in the number of seminaries in Hong Kong to twenty-seven in 2001 from seventeen in 1997. Many of these seminaries are funded by their representative overseas denomination, usually located in the United States. At an organizational meeting for one of these new seminary start-ups, a leader specifically said one of the main reasons for developing this new seminary is "to create loyalty to our respective theological tradition by training our own people."

A HISTORY OF THE PROBLEM: A POLITICAL ECONOMY OF A PRIVILEGED CHURCH

Elites, Middlemen and the Church (1842–1949)[9]

Britain acquired Hong Kong Island along with five other treaty ports through the Treaty of Nanjing signed in 1842 following the first Opium War (1839–1842) with China. The British desired Hong Kong, not for gaining local resources nor for expanding British territory, but primarily for a protected base for trade and capital expansion into China. An important aspect of Hong Kong's history is this perspective of Hong

---

9. What follows is greatly indebted to conversations with Carl Smith and the argument he makes in *Chinese Christians: Elites, Middlemen, and the Church in Hong Kong* (1985).

Kong as a "stepping stone" between China and the world. Hong Kong represented an ideal port at the edge of an important center of trade in South China, the Canton delta region.

When foreign occupation began on January 26, 1841, there were only a few fishing villages as well as various floating populations of outcasts, pirates, and other vagrants seeking refuge for one reason or another from Chinese laws and customs. The local population has been estimated at under 5,000 leading historians later to refer to Hong Kong as a "barren rock" when the British arrived (Carroll 1999,18; Smith 1970). Hong Kong's development could not have happened apart from the collaboration of the migrants it attracted as a "free port."

Throughout Hong Kong's history, migrants brought important labor and capital. The social composition of these migrants made for a unique colonial experience and created a "Hong Kong mentality" that locals began to consciously identify as they faced the return to Chinese sovereignty. The border crossings and the meaning of the border between Hong Kong and China remain an important factor in the making of Hong Kong. The Chinese that came to Hong Kong were those on the margins of society within Mainland China. The incoming migrants were of low social status (not gentry), willing to take risks, and interested more in making money than settling down. Many came seeking refuge, and overall they held a transient mentality. Hong Kong was not "home," and their intentions were not to make it "home." They had little to lose and became adept at borrowing, adjusting, and taking advantage of any available resource. The migrating Chinese created their own new social structure, one where elite status was based on wealth rather than on knowledge of Chinese literary classics (gentry). It was common for the new elite to later buy themselves these degrees. This is to say that this new social composition was willing to compromise, change, and adapt to gain new forms of power that were unavailable to them in "traditional" China.

The dominant historical narrative has attributed Hong Kong's success to its colonial government and policies of socio-political non-intervention and laissez-faire economics. Although this has been shown to be inaccurately one-sided, one cannot ignore the influence of these policies on shaping Hong Kong peoples' decisions. While it may be a myth that the markets and society operated freely apart from government or colonial influences, it is important to recognize the extent to which the idea of laissez-faire economics, a policy of non-intervention and free market capitalism, came to embody the values demanding ultimate allegiance and later the "officially sanctioned historiographic position maintained by mainland Chinese officials" (Ngo 1999, 135).

The dominant concern of those developing the new Hong Kong was to make money, whether colonial or Chinese. The new Chinese provided labor to build the new infrastructure (small industry) as well as fill the important role of compradors (middlemen or the new elite) who facilitated trade between foreigners and China. This interesting and unique mix of actors and structural constraints/opportunities is what sets Hong Kong apart from other colonial experiences in Asia. So how do Christians, churches, and Christianity fit into this picture of capital expansion?

Mainland China's population has for a long time represented a challenge to Christian missions. China's government and people have made it difficult for foreigners to operate within China. The first Protestant missionary to China, Robert Morrison, arrived in 1807 and immediately found it difficult to gain entry. In order to gain access to China, Morrison as well as others who would follow worked as translators for British merchants (East India Company). The missionaries offered abilities to mediate trade between English and Chinese speakers. They were the first middlemen or compradors. Given these early difficulties, missionaries welcomed the cession of these treaty ports and the safe haven Hong Kong provided to pursue the missionization of China. Just days after the British took possession of Hong Kong in 1841, a party of missionaries came from Macau to Hong Kong to examine prospects for mission. They saw little promise for building churches locally, but they saw a tremendous advantage to have a base so close to China.

The missionary enterprise did not begin until it was officially ceded to the British in 1842 when Issachar J. Roberts, a Baptist missionary, became the first missionary to take up permanent residence in Hong Kong. A large part of the first missionary presence was to provide services for the foreign population. But there soon was a growing need to establish Chinese churches as migrants came in from China as well as for the Chinese converts missionaries brought with them from other Southeast Asian locations.

One of the most important factors in the development of Hong Kong was the churches early development of English-language education. The church was interested in educating Chinese Christians in order to facilitate the translation of Christian literature into Chinese and to further serve in the mission process in China. The product of this education served a far greater demand than just the church. These students found that their newly acquired education could pay well in the world of trade and commerce. As Carl Smith, a Hong Kong Historian, describes it:

> They created a man who stood between two cultures, a man who was not altogether at home in either. He was not wholly in the Chinese Model, nor was he altogether Western. This dual aspect of his thought and outlook enabled him to fill a needed place in the meeting of the Chinese nation with foreigners promoting trade and commerce. The foreign merchant needed a Chinese to supervise the Chinese side of his business. Chinese merchants trading with foreigners needed a Chinese who understood the foreigner and who could speak his language. The Governments of both China and Hong Kong needed translators and interpreters ... This group of Chinese interpreters, compradors, advisors to officials and Government, and men in various professions created a distinct culture in the China coast cities. (Smith 1985, 10–11)

This group of people that Smith refers to became the elite in Hong Kong's emerging social organization where wealth and bilingual ability provided the important means to achieve that position. The church became the "educational contractor" for the government (Karsen 1980, 6). The church run schools helped to produce the new elite of Hong Kong, working as civil servants in government and compradors in business (Smith 1985; Kwok 1996, 94). By 1950, seventeen of the top twenty secondary schools were run by the Christian community (Kwok 1994). By the end of the 1950s, "of the 30 most famous secondary schools, with the exception of five directly run by the government, all were run by churches or church organizations. Until the 1960s, these schools monopolized almost entirely the admissions into the University of Hong Kong, the only university in the territory until 1962" (Kwok 1997, 4). Christianity from the West was pivotal in shaping the value system of these new elite. The neo-liberal values embodied in laissez-faire economics were not questioned, and the new elite as well as the new church adapted itself to the unique social and economic conditions of Hong Kong. The church run education system helped to form individuals who would fit into this new social, economic, and political configuration called Hong Kong.

Church Growth and Organized Dependence on the State (1950–1982)

When I inquired about the values and characteristics of Hong Kong people, I was consistently told the stories of Hong Kong people's pragmatism, strength, and resilience in facing crises. The "China factor" consistently stood at the center of these crises. The making and remaking of Hong Kong in one sense is the process of adapting to historical and social forces at work between the borders of Hong Kong, China and the world. The year 1949 begins one of the significant periods of crisis that has shaped Hong Kong. Mao Zedong defeated the nationalists, and the communist government of the People's Republic of China was successfully established. Because of various natural disasters (floods & famine), war between the nationalists and communists, and finally the victory of Mao, hundreds of thousands Chinese refugees flooded Hong Kong. By 1952 Hong Kong's population had reached 2 million, and the previous flow of people and goods between China and Hong Kong became severely restricted effectively creating a significant border or rather boundary.

A few years later, because of China's support of North Korea in the Korean War, the United Nations imposed a trade embargo on the purchase of goods from China through Hong Kong. Thus, Hong Kong was further separated from the world and was now faced with the challenge of creating a new economy. It quickly transformed itself from being an entrepôt to a manufacturing center. No longer able to sustain itself primarily as "middlemen" of trade, Hong Kong adapted by industrializing itself and marketing plastic flowers, clothing, and later electronics for the world. The flow of capital especially from the Shanghai refugees sparked the building of local industry. What did this shift in the political-economy mean for the church?

Some historians have said that Hong Kong's history begins in 1949, and in a similar vein, it is said, "in real terms, the Christian church in Hong Kong only began to develop in the 1950s" (Kwok 1996, 95). The significance of this perspective points to a radical shift in social organization and processes brought on by what has been termed the "China factor." In 1949, China officially declared itself off limits to foreign missionaries. Since 1807, mission groups primarily focused resources and vision on China, whereas Hong Kong served merely as an important base to operate from (since 1842). When China closed, mission groups as well as Chinese Christians had to decide what to do with their resources. For the most part, the churches' resources followed the flood of migrants and their capital to Hong Kong. Over thirty American mission groups not already present in Hong Kong began mission work among these refugees (Kwong 2000, 42; Barrett 1982, 362). Hong Kong was a social services disaster. The government did not have the resources to respond to this crisis partly because of its non-intervention policies. The government welcomed wholeheartedly the church as its partner in providing emergency relief and pioneering social services development. The Hong Kong Christian Council was organized in 1954 partly to help organize and coordinate emergency relief efforts supplied by churches (Kwong 2000, 52; Kwok 1997, 6).

By the 1960s, already successful in relief work, the church moved on to providing education for all these marginal Hong Kong children who did not have access to education. With the help of the church the government was finally able to offer nine years of free and compulsory education in 1978. The partnership between church and government expanded with the government offering land and capital if the church would provide the human resources needed to build and manage the schools. Again the church played an important part in providing education to a new group of China immigrants that provided them with important social capital to achieve economic success and elite status.

This partnership developed further in the areas of social services and hospitals. In the 1960s, mission groups started small clinics, and local churches collaborated to build the United Christian Hospital. Built in the Kwun Tung Industrial area, this was an important project to connect the church with the grassroots community. Kwok Nai-wang and the Hong Kong Christian Institute determined that today the church provides 60 percent of the community's social services, 50 percent of the secondary schools, 40 percent of the primary schools, 30 percent of the kindergartens, and 20 percent of its hospitals (Kwok 1997, 3). This period marks the first of two periods of major church growth. Evangelical, mainline protestant, and Catholic churches all grew significantly in terms of members, institutions, and material resources (Kwong Chun0wah 2000, 52; Barrett 1982, 362). A local sociologist shared:

> In the 1960s and 1970s, becoming a Christian was viewed as a means to social mobility, moving up. The church was viewed as a good place to go and improve your English skills. It was a path

to become the middle class. These were hard times for Hong Kong people. Only 2 percent of Hong Kong people could enter a university. So, there were limited opportunities for social mobility. The Catholic and Protestant schools were viewed as the best schools and one the best opportunities for upward mobility. So, parents would often become Christians to get their children into the best schools. This is changing now. But it shows that Hong Kong people are very practical.

By the late 1960s, Hong Kong had grown economically, considered now as one of the four little dragons of Asia (capitalist success stories: Korea, Taiwan, Singapore, Hong Kong). The church grew with the economy and was by the early 1970s composed largely of middle class educated professionals (Karsen 1980, 30). The rise of this local affluence coupled with the budget constraints facing overseas mission groups caused most of the foreign mission organizations to pull their resources out of Hong Kong during this period.

The majority of church leaders identify this period as the time of Christianity's indigenization in Hong Kong. One could argue as do a minority of local voices that Hong Kong does not have an indigenous church. The measure for indigenization by the majority is compliance with the Three-Self principles: self-governing, self-supporting, and self-propagating. According to these measures which date back to nineteenth century mission theory, Hong Kong did become indigenous. But has Christianity in Hong Kong truly become localized? This is a question that Joseph Kuang asks particularly in terms of local theological meanings (Kuang 1993, 1994, 2003). The Hong Kong "crisis" of decolonization provided an opportunity to reflect on this issue. Kuang argues that Hong Kong still remains "theologically colonized." My research points to the same conclusion.

Locals took over the role of leadership in many cases and more significantly many church institutions became dependent upon the government for financing its operations. Missionaries remained and still remain in Hong Kong, especially those tied to smaller evangelical and independent churches. It is extremely difficult to relinquish control. I call this ecclesiastical hegemony. Still, the majority church became dependent upon the government. Chan Shun-hing, a sociologist, describes the relationship between the church and government since 1950 as a "channeled partnership" (Chan 1999). While looking through the government archives in Kwun Tong, Chan found a letter from Bishop Ronald Hall to the secretary of education written in the 1950s. Hall said boldly that the government could depend upon the Christians. He asked for the government to place its trust (i.e., funds) in Christian organizations and not with the Chinese religious groups because they were all communist leftists. The secretary replied to this letter giving his full support and agreement to Hall and the Christian institutions. "This was the relationship of channeled partnership" says Chan. Sir David Trench, former governor of Hong Kong, said in 1970, "Indeed, I can think of few societies where there exists such close and harmonious collaboration between the government and such a variety of Christian bodies... who have an immense influence for good" (1970, 5).

The church has enjoyed many special privileges, such as large government subsidies and cheap lands (often free) that have now become prime properties. When western mission organizations pulled their money out in the 1960s because of new wealth in Hong Kong, the church immediately became reliant on financial support from the government and private business. During the 1960s and 1970s the government offered land and money to churches in return for the staff and direction to create an education system in Hong Kong. In 1981, several church leaders met with the government to secure legislation whereby the government would grant land at nil premium (free) in return for social services. The church developed an elite status and wealthy position in the established order.

THE 1997 CRISIS: POLITICIZATION OF THE CHURCH AND INSTITUTIONAL SURVIVAL (1984–1997)

What I have tried to demonstrate so far is the extent to which the church secured itself a privileged position within society by the 1980s. This is important to show because one then sees what is at stake for the church as it faces a shift in the relations of power brought on by the perceived crisis of the 1997 handover. At stake for the church were its considerable influence and control over vast local resources and its future role and control of that enterprise into China with Deng's changing policies. At another level, the future of the church would depend upon the emigration decision of individual households whose concerns included religious freedom but more so continued economic prosperity.

As the terms of the Sino-British Joint Declaration, ratified in 1984, were negotiated, the Hong Kong people became more fully conscious of the uncertainty of their future. The discourse and practice of the church reflects what was happening across social domains in Hong Kong. The society as a whole was making attempts to "tally the 'credit card' of colonial rule, to explore the prospects of the local consciousness in withstanding alien ideological and political meaning systems, or to come to terms, at an intellectual or emotional level, with one's experience in Hong Kong" (Wong 1998, 1). That Hong Kong was "borrowed space" and that its people were living on "borrowed time" was no surprise.

Britain obtained the territories of Hong Kong through the "unequal" treaties of 1842, 1860, and 1898. China never recognized these treaties as legitimate since they were obtained by coercion and "gunboat diplomacy." It was the leasing of the New Territories in 1898 for ninety-nine years that really set the final date for colonial Hong Kong, July 1, 1997.

When China "officially" declared in September 1982 its intention to resume sovereignty over Hong Kong in 1997, the public finally began to face this reality. Britain began talks with China to negotiate the terms of the transfer of sovereignty. These talks ended in 1984 with the Joint Declaration on the future of Hong Kong signed by both parties and with the exclusion of local Hong Kong participation. Hong Kong would become a "highly autonomous" Special Administrative Region of China in 1997 according to Deng Xiaoping's plan of "one country, two systems." Hong Kong people were promised that they would continue to rule Hong Kong except in "foreign and defense affairs." Most important to Hong Kong people, the Joint Declaration guaranteed that Hong Kong's "previous capitalist system and lifestyle" would remain unchanged for fifty years.

For Hong Kong Christians, the Joint Declaration and the Basic Law both guarantee that Hong Kong's religious freedom will be protected based on the principles of the "three mutuals" (*san hu*): non-subordination (*hu bu lishu*), non-interference (*hu bu ganshe*), and mutual respect (*huxiang zunzhong*). The church in Hong Kong was guaranteed autonomy in all local matters. But the Hong Kong church was also to give China the same autonomy especially with regards to the heavy missionization from Hong Kong Christian organizations.

The terms appear very clear, but the interpretation of the terms always creates ambiguity and tension. The churches' earlier concerns in the 1980s have materialized recently over the practice of Falungong in Hong Kong. Falungong was made illegal in China and labeled a subversive sect and political group posing a threat to China's national security. According to the Sino-British agreements, China could exercise power within Hong Kong in order to protect national security. An attempt was made to ban the group in Hong Kong, but local protestors dissuaded legislation efforts. This incident raised the question regarding what makes a group political versus religious. Although the Falungong continue to exercise religious freedom, their activities are severely restricted. The message received by local church leaders was that their religious freedoms were contingent on their political activities. And more troubling was that China ultimately controlled the interpretation of these terms and laws.

The early 1980s marks an important shift in the theological perspective and priority of the Hong Kong church, particularly when formal dialogues between Britain and China were initiated in 1982 and society began facing the historical challenge of 1997. At the 1986 HKCC conference they decided, "in light of these drastic changes, the mission strategies laid down at the last mission conference require reconsideration and adjustment." The issues that 1997 presented dominated the consultation. Hong Kong theologically became for the first time preoccupied with politics and nation building. The church for the first time became concerned with political issues such as the relationship between church and state, the freedom of religion post-1997, the potential disappearance of privileges and resources received from the British colonial Hong Kong government, and future relationships with its new colonial master China.

At the same time that Hong Kong faced the reality of the 1997 handover, China's new open door policy (1979) brought Hong Kong people back in contact with mainland Chinese people. What many Hong Kong people soon realized when the doors were reopened was how different they were now from those living in China. There were fears of these "backward country bumpkins" flooding Hong Kong and causing an economic drain. Many of Hong Kong's people held stories of suffering in China from which they escaped. There were fears of renewed political oppression. These issues among others were perceived as a crisis to be faced.

Two important documents representing the majority of Hong Kong churches begin with the recognition of a perceived crisis: "At this critical moment of historical change, the Protestant Church in Hong Kong wishes to express its deepest concern about the future of religious freedom in Hong Kong and to make the following statement" (1984 Manifesto) and "The 1997 issue has created deep concern and anxiety among the people of Hong Kong" (1984, The Convictions). In Chinese, the word for crisis means both danger and opportunity, and this is how the church at large related to the circumstances of the "handover" crisis (Kwok 1996, 6). The common response of most church leaders was that we are "cautiously optimistic."

When the HKCC held its mission consultation in 1980, the 1997 handover issue had not yet surfaced (HKCC 1982). At that time, the church determined its major mission priorities to be establishing relations with the church in China and outreach to the poor in Hong Kong (HKCC 1986, 2). For nearly all churches in Hong Kong, discussion of new opportunities for mission and relations to churches within China dominated conversations since the normalizing of China's religious policies in 1979. With the death of Mao Zedong, the end of the Cultural Revolution, and a new plan of economic modernization under Deng Xiaoping's leadership, came the reopening of the boundary between Hong Kong and China.

Hong Kong awakened to its historical role as a stepping-stone into China. Again, foreign money and groups came to Hong Kong in a frenzy to penetrate the China mission field. Illegal Bible smuggling was one of the hot political and theological topics around which was attached the anti-communist rhetoric. Churches argued over whom to side with: the illegal underground house churches or the government sanctioned Three-Self Patriotic Movement (TSPM) churches. Generally more conservative groups were anti-communistic and therefore anti-TSPM. The HKCC and the more mainline churches chose to establish relations with the TSPM church in China and in March 1979 made their first official visit.

But it wasn't until the Chinese Christian delegation visited Hong Kong in March 1981 that a firm and continued relation began to develop. The implementation of the principles of "non-subordination, non-interference, and mutual respect" guaranteed in the Basic Law became a challenge as Hong Kong and International churches considered missions to Mainland China and relationships with Mainland Churches. Prior to the negotiations over 1997, the majority of Hong Kong churches strongly supported the illegal house church movement in Mainland China. But slowly as the implications of 1997 were considered, "Hong Kong's theology has moved northward (Nanjing)" remarked one local theologian. Nanjing is the location of the headquarters of the official (legal) churches of China: the Chinese Christian Council (CCC) and the Three Self Patriotic Movement (TSPM). The Hong Kong church has officially come to support the TSPM in order to facilitate access to China's people and churches.

Those who do not support the TSPM churches keep quiet about it and work underground. One of the largest mission groups working with the illegal house church moved its headquarters to Taiwan prior to 1997. The HKCRM survey recently showed 41.9 percent of Hong Kong Churches have regular contacts and ministries with churches in Mainland China. From my interviews I would estimate that a much higher number of churches have ministry contacts within Mainland China. Those churches that remain connected with house churches communicated to me that they do not disclose this information to the public and many times not even to their own congregation in order to not cause trouble. The Mainland China factor remains one of the more important factors that continues to shape theological practice in Hong Kong and its perception of the 1997 handover as a crisis.

From a 1996 study of religion in Hong Kong by a researcher from Beijing, Xue Zheng concludes, "religion (in Hong Kong) is influenced by hostile international forces which have constantly exploited Hong Kong and exploited religion as a base from which to penetrate our country (China)." Therefore, he continues, religion in Hong Kong will need "continued long term vigilance" (Xue 1996). This is the political-economic backdrop of the following chapters.

4

Unholy Alliance— Theologies of Dominance and Crisis

INTRODUCTION

ON THE EVENING OF July 9, 1997, I sat in our apartment in Fanling, Hong Kong, watching the news of the day's events. I watched as Chief Executive Tung Chee-hwa gave a speech to the Ninth Assembly of the Lutheran World Federation (LWF) at the newly built Exhibition and Convention Centre where just nine days earlier British officials handed Hong Kong back over to China. The development of this story was an important turning point during my field research when I began to ask new questions and see important connections concerning the changing structural relations of power, Christianity, and the political economy. Tung pledged to preserve religious freedom in the new Special Administrative Region (SAR) of China "so long as they (churches and religious organizations) fall within the law."

The story begins more than a year earlier. The Lutheran World Federation (LWF) assembly almost did not happen. In February 1996, the New China News Agency (*Xinhua*), China's de facto embassy in Hong Kong, asked the Lutherans to postpone their assembly although a space had already been rented and plans already set in place. One stated cause for China's concern was the planned presence of a delegation from Taiwan. Eventually, the controversy was settled, and the Lutherans were allowed to hold their conference under the conditions that no national flags (i.e., Taiwan's national flag) would be on display. The international conference included discussions on human rights and religious freedoms that caused a controversy when local representatives of Hong Kong churches opposed two resolutions, one criticizing China's human rights record and the other stating concern over the right of abode of children of local residents born in Mainland China. Local church representatives argued in the assembly's last day of discussion on July 16 that the criticism would be "a great insult for the Chinese, considered unfriendly, and hurt the feelings of Chinese people around the world." The director of the LWF said that they removed the resolutions later because "the assembly respects the wishes of the local churches."

On the morning of July 24, I interviewed Kwok Nai-wang, former director of the Hong Kong Christian Institute (HKCI). I no more than introduced my research agenda before he reached for a newspaper and asked, "Did you read the South China Morning Post today?" The story he was concerned with ran in the South China Morning Post as *Lutheran Church Drops Criticism of Beijing* (Chan 1997). Kwok continued with his diatribe: "This is the mentality of the institutional church leaders ... The survival syndrome has made them weak ... They have built up an empire, not with the churches' money, but with someone else's, the government and business tycoons. The institutional church wants to be a part of the establishment. These are the three groups: the business tycoons are the bosses, the government is the major servant, and the church is the minor partner serving this unholy alliance. The church sanctions it. This is what Emily Lau, who was a legislative councilor until this last June, calls the 'unholy alliance.'" What was this "unholy alliance" that Emily Lau wrote about in the *Far Eastern Economic Review* back in 1987? This became an important question in the development of the research project.

"AN UNHOLY ALLIANCE"—CHURCH AND STATE CO-OPTED BY BIG BUSINESS

The liberals fear that their aspirations for a democratic system of government after 1997 may be stifled by what is commonly called 'an unholy alliance' among the conservative church leaders, business interests and the communists. Political observers say Peking has neutralized the potential power of the church by co-opting its leaders into the decision-making process.

—Emily Lau, "An Unholy Alliance"

Church leaders, the government authorities (also including those in Beijing) and business tycoons have given birth to an 'unholy alliance.' This alliance is beneficial to all parties concerned. Those who hold political power and the economic power are pleased to have the sanction and support of the church leaders who supposedly have the moral power.

—Kwok Nai-wang, *Hong Kong Braves 1997*

The accusation Emily Lau made in 1987 of the Hong Kong churches' complicity in the political and economic structure of power emerges out of a particular concern for political reforms as the 1997 handover approached. The future of Hong Kong was decided through negotiations between the British and Chinese governments (1982–1984) and enshrined in the Sino-British Joint Declaration all without the involvement of Hong Kong citizens. When the British government published in November 1984 a white paper on "The Development of Representative Government," a small group of Hong Kong people became concerned about the lack of democracy and representative government, including Emily Lau who returned to Hong Kong as a journalist for the *Far Eastern Economic Review* in 1984 to involve herself in this very issue. When Lau posed a critical question to Margaret Thatcher, she responded: "Everyone in Hong Kong is happy with the agreement. You may be a solitary exception" (Lau 1997, 36). When the first direct elections were held in 1991 for eighteen legislators of the total sixty-member Legislative Council (LegCo), Lau ran as a democratic candidate and won with overwhelming popular support.

A number of Christians branded as "liberals" joined democracy activists to fight for a more representative government and for the rights of all Hong Kong people. As this small group of Christians spoke out for democratic reforms, they found opposition from two influential bodies—the business and church community. The business and church elite decidedly became "pro-China" after 1984, a community that considered its relationship with its British colonizer in positive terms. The majority of church leaders, concerned with their own survival, have chosen what Lau calls a "conservative" approach to 1997 by avoiding confrontation and maintaining a low profile. This conservative majority includes both mainline and evangelical churches.

Conservative evangelical churches overall remain silent about all social and political issues. Conservative mainline churches cooperate in the building of the new SAR by sending representatives when asked and refraining from making any statements of criticism. The theologies of the "unholy alliance" inform practices, policies, and actions that legitimize or "morally sanction" the structural relations of power within Hong Kong's political-economy which further benefit the business elite. This research finds Emily Lau's critical description of an emergent "unholy alliance" as a result of the 1997 handover further to be descriptive of the longer history of Hong Kong Christendom allied with an elitist social structure, laissez-faire economics, colonial politics, and conservative theology.

LAISSEZ-FAIRE ECONOMIC COLONIALISM

Eric Wolf notes that crises "magnify and display structure and themes that might remain more muted and veiled among peoples who are less assertive in their ways of life" (1999, 17). This is the case in Hong Kong. As 1997 came to be viewed by the public as an impending crisis, the structural relations of power were more clearly revealed as those in power concerned themselves with remaining in power. The complicity of the church at large in support of a business elite and an economic way of life that managed the political transition of 1997, not only continues with China but also emerged out of a colonial way of life that China was most interested in retaining. As one historian writes, the promise to keep politics separate from economics in order to protect the free market becomes the "officially sanctioned historiographic position maintained by mainland Chinese officials . . . that allows the in-coming power interlocutors to claim special privileges under the new regime as the British hongs had done under colonial rule" (Ngo 1999, 135).

Emily Lau's description of an "unholy alliance" is not entirely new. I heard Richard Hughes' 1968 observation quoted often around Hong Kong: "Power in Hong Kong, it has been said, resides in the Jockey Club, Jardine Matheson, the Hong Kong and Shanghai Bank, and the Governor—in that order" (Hughes 1968, 23). This study finds that the institutional church follows right in line after big business and the executive government. At the first Consultation on the Mission of the Church in Hong Kong in 1970, the Governor, Sir David Trench, said, "an over concern with good works should not be allowed to degenerate into something like political polemics" and that the "Church's proper role in society" is shaping individual morality and personal ethics (*South China*

Morning Post, January 20, 1970). This warning from the British government sounds no different from the current warnings coming from China regarding the role of Christian churches in society.

Emily Lau wonders why the church in Hong Kong shows no interest in the struggle for democracy, especially in light of its great organizational power, when this has been the case in the Philippines, South Korea and other Asian countries (Lau 1987, 23). The institutional church, as well as the vast majority of Christians who belong to the church, does not share with other Asian countries the disdain for the colonial way of life (Lee 1999, 157). Joseph Kuang, a Hong Kong theologian, criticizes the local church for maintaining a "colonial theology" (Kuang 1993). While the 1997 issue could have provided the agenda for "theological decolonization" in Hong Kong, the church continues to live on "borrowed theologies" (Kuang 1993, 17). Hong Kong churches and Christians would rather follow the theologies and trends of the West. Although a leading Japanese theologian, Kosuke Koyama, wrote in 1974 that Hong Kong's theological agenda should embrace the issue of 1997, it took eight more years for Hong Kong Christians to address the issue laments Kuang.

A theological movement across "Asia" connects "Asian theologies" based on a common frame of reference called the "critical Asian principles," but Hong Kong does not fit because of its unique colonial experience (Wong 1997b; Kuang 1996; Lee 1996a, 1999b; Kwan 1998, 1999a, 1999b). "The Hong Kong experience and the Asian theological movement seem to find each other irrelevant" (Kwan 1999b, 261). Wong defends Hong Kong Christians, including herself: "As a Hong Kong modern western educated person I find it hard to identify with the suffering 'Asian.'" In Wong's doctoral dissertation, she challenges the unified "Asian" theologies that limit the subject of theology to anti-colonialism, nation-building, liberation, and the poor. "Contrary to the national woman or the poor woman in Asian theological discourses, people in a city of uncertainties and anxieties like Hong Kong do not look for a national liberator or agents of revolutionary changes, but to themselves in maximizing their creativity and productivity" (Wong 1997, 280). In a comparison of "post-colonial" Hong Kong with post-exilic Trito-Isaiah, Archie Lee affirms "co-operation with Babylon (China) as a way of survival" and posits "co-existence with Babylon (China) as safer than resistance and opposition" (Lee 1999b, 171). The theologies of largely middle class western educated Hong Kong Christians will continue to focus on private spiritual interests in order to maintain economic prosperity and political stability. Democracy from this perspective is viewed as a threat to neo-liberal capitalist values of free and global economic markets. Those who benefited under the British colonial system will continue to benefit by "kowtowing" to the new sovereignty, Beijing, as long as capitalist values shape all others. The church hopes it will survive by continuing to cooperate with the capitalists as it always has in Hong Kong.

The majority of Hong Kong people were in agreement that British colonialism ought to come to an end in 1997. But the majority were also equally concerned that the "stability and prosperity" they enjoyed under British colonialism might come to an end. The Sino-British Joint Declaration (1984) and the Basic Law (1989), Hong Kong's constitution, both were conceived to protect for fifty years this primary concern—Hong Kong's capitalistic way of life. This is the primary meaning of "one country, two systems." One theologian has asked whether Hong Kong simply experienced "re-colonization" rather than "post-colonization" (Chia 1999; Kwok 1996; Kuang 1993, 1994; Kwan 1999). While the majority of Hong Kong theologians and church leaders embrace positively the idea of a "post-colonial" Hong Kong, Chia asks if they have missed a more subtle internal domination that is economic rather than political in nature. Chia compares what happened in "post-colonial" Malaysia with Hong Kong.

> In a postcolonial experience, it is precisely because of continuity of these colonization elements—culture that was previously experienced and learnt through colonization as imposed by the colonizer on the colonized, by means of education and domination—that even though when proceeded into a postcolonial era, the formerly colonized people, in their conscious or unconscious, intentional or unintentional way, continued to behave like their colonizers in transforming a postcolonial state into an opportunity for 'internal colonization'; that is, a colonization of their own people . . . The people (or rather the capitalists) in Hong Kong have mastered the skill of colonization through economic power. (Chia 1999, 177)

The theologies promulgated by the majority of churches in Hong Kong accommodate the values of the economic system by focusing on private spirituality, individual morality, and an otherworldly salvation.

The dialogue among Hong Kong theologians does suggest that the political-economic context of Hong Kong shapes social relations across all social domains including religious. Richard Rosecrance describes Hong Kong as the paramount "virtual state," a model for the twenty-first century (1999). This description of Hong Kong helps one understand better the theologies of Hong Kong Christians and their primary interests. In a "virtual state," local labor and capital are less important than their flows, and land is less important than knowledge and services. The protection of territory through military or political dominance is not as important because of the focus on the mobility of capital, labor, and information. This is reflected in Hong Kong's GDP: 83 percent from services as opposed to eight percent from manufacturing. Since Deng's reforms in China in the late 1970s, Hong Kong has moved its manufacturing demands to southern China. The primary interest of Hong Kong people is simply to gain more of the world's output. Virtual states like Hong Kong, as opposed to nation-states, develop partnerships between the market and state in order to accommodate each other's interests. Most important to this discussion of virtual states are the shared values and norms that flow across territorial borders to insure stability and economic prosperity. The "unholy alliance" in Hong Kong as described by Lau, the co-operation of business, state, and church, suggests a "laissez-faire colonialism" exists to protect the economic interests of the parties involved.

CAPITAL-FRIENDLY CHRISTIANITY AND MONETIZED THEOLOGIES

Studies by social scientists show that Hong Kong people value individual freedom, hard work, competition, social stability, and equality of opportunity (Lau 1982; Lau and Kuan 1988; Wong and Lui 1993; Baker 1995; Watson 1997; Mathews 1998). In a *South China Morning Post* article in December 2000, Hong Kong was listed as one of the world's most capitalistic countries. Cost-benefit analysis and instrumental calculation provide the moral basis of society and the churches' theology accommodates it. "How to relate to others seems to have been largely determined by the norms of the free market," laments one theologian (Kwan 1999, 369). Kwan borrows from Habermas to say that Hong Kong's "life world" or shared system of meaning has been colonized by the "market economy" or society's administrative and economic system coordinated by money and power. "Christians in Hong Kong behave no differently than do most citizens, totally secular and materialistic" (Kwok 1997, 26). Chan Shun-hing in his study of a local church found that Hong Kong Christians held the same values as the local population: "concern for material wealth and social status, pragmatic, instrumental and rationalistic attitude toward traditional values."

Further, "Chinese values are viewed as a cultural resource to be tapped and utilized according to instrumental consideration" (Chan 1995, 256). These findings are no surprise as this happens in most places around the world and through Christian history. Another sociologist writes, "Traditions are not necessarily treasured affectively for their intrinsic goodness. Traditions are being selectively preserved mainly on their extrinsic usefulness in pursuing economic goals" (King 1987, 16–17). The same could be said of Hong Kong Churches' appropriation of Christian traditions and values.

While visiting the Chinese University of Hong Kong (CUHK) library, I met a local pastor reading through a stack of books on the theology of John Wesley. I found this curious for a number of reasons. Wesley and other historical theological figures were absent from the Christian bookstores and pastors' libraries I had visited. Also, those churches that self identify as Wesleyan theologically in Hong Kong are a minority. Further, I did not associate eighteenth century Wesley with the pragmatic decision-making I saw within the church. Pastors were reading the latest church growth techniques produced largely from the West. So when I saw him taking a break, I asked if I could bother him with a few questions. Why are you reading about John Wesley? He smiled and warmed right up to conversation. He graduated long ago from Chung Chi College (CUHK) and is now finishing a degree he started awhile back at Emory's Chandler School of Theology in the United States. His last paper assignment was on the theology of John Wesley. I said I was a bit surprised to see someone in Hong Kong reading John Wesley. He agreed and said he only learned about Wesley's theology from a guest lecturer from Britain back when he was in seminary at CUHK. I asked about Hong Kong theologies. He said Hong Kong does not have an affinity with any one theology. "Hong Kong's theology is practical theology and for me, these books on John Wesley's theology are practical. We borrow from many as we find useful. Hong Kong Christians are pragmatic. We use what works." He continued to explain why he found

John Wesley useful for practical Christianity in Hong Kong. I found this kind of utilitarian Christianity focused on church growth very common among Hong Kong pastors and Christians. This explains the ease with which pastors commonly move from one denominational affiliation to another. Pragmatism drives their theological agenda and practice.

A local theologian observed that Hong Kong culture is about "the power of money" and "commercialization" (Kung 1995, 220). There is a "Hong Kong dream" and it doesn't look much different from the "American Dream." The "Hong Kong Dream" is captured as reality in the success story of Li Ka-shing, characterized as hard working and boldly intelligent. His story of rags to riches, from plastic flowers to property magnate, is one that the majority of Hong Kong people believe is possible for anyone. The private and public worlds for Christians are separated such that Li ka-shing can provide a model of salvation for this world just as Jesus provides salvation for another. Aihwa Ong, professor at the University of California (Berkeley), spoke at the City University of Hong Kong in June 2001 about her research on the effects of neo-liberal practices on the meaning of citizenship in three "globalizing Asian cities"— Singapore, Kuala Lumpur, and Hong Kong. Aihwa Ong discovered in Singapore that Muslims are adapting Islam to become more capital friendly in order to accommodate the emerging sphere of market values. This is the similar to Christianity in Hong Kong. The theological practice and discourse of Hong Kong Christians accommodates neo-liberal economic practices and values.

Christians and churches in Hong Kong have survived and even prospered by restricting the role of religion to acceptable social domains. For mainline denominations and the Catholic Church this means continuing to provide services to the community. For evangelical churches this means focusing on evangelism and discipleship. The practice and meaning of Christianity is restricted to individual, spiritual, and internal affairs of the church. Hong Kong Christians can embrace the slogan of all Hong Kong people since 1985, "prosperity and stability," because they "focus on the individual and the mind" (Chow 1995, 294). The Christian message in Hong Kong is understood as relevant to only the private or spiritual dimension of life allowing for the ideology and values associated with laissez-faire economics to rule the public dimensions of life. The values of pragmatism, utility, self-interest, and rationalism that structure social relations coexist with values of love and sacrifice that are believed to shape the affairs of one's soul privately now but corporately one day in heaven.

Hong Kong's idea of contextualization, says a Hong Kong sociologist, "focuses on evangelism to particular Hong Kong needs." This focus on evangelism is what makes the majority of Hong Kong churches' theology, including mainline churches, conservative, says one church leader. The church stays away from political and economic issues for the sake of stability and prosperity. Ko Ting-ming's study of political participation of ministers in Hong Kong implicates theology as the most important factor for non-participation (Ko 1998, 2000). Christian theological practice and discourse in a powerful way protects the structural relations of power that shape social relations. Problems arise when a Christian minority questions these limitations by asserting their faith in politics and the marketplace. Silence on politics and economics has proven advantageous for the church and for Christians to protect their interests. What are the interests at stake?

"INTEREST" AND "VALUE" WITHIN THE CHRISTIANITY COMMUNITY

Locally, there is a vast enterprise including land, buildings, salaries, and subsidies that churches have no interest in losing. One evangelical leader of a large denomination told me that they are not complicit in Lau's description of an "unholy alliance" because they do not take government monies. Yet the agreement made in 1981 to grant churches land at nil premium in exchange for a social service largely benefited evangelical groups interested in church growth in the developing satellite towns. The most important resources for all churches are the church members themselves who provide tithes and contributions. A church from this same evangelical denomination spent HK$70 million in 1994 to purchase ten thousand square feet in a building on top of a MTR Station in a busy district largely with local member donations (Kwok 1994, 92). One of the largest evangelical congregations in Hong Kong is in the middle of building a new church at the cost of HK$2 billion also largely from member donations they tell me proudly.

When I asked one evangelical minister if he ever preaches on the topic of what Jesus said about money, he replied, "we cannot preach on this subject because it might upset our members." I heard only one sermon on money during my field research. Based on James 4:13–17, the minister interpreted the passage to mean "there is more to life than making money." The minister continued that money would not secure salvation and eternal life after death. The preacher footnoted his theology of money by saying, "don't worry now, I'm not trying to say there is anything wrong with making money. It's just that money can't buy everything. That's why we need Jesus." The passage that he chose to exegete stops conveniently just before chapter five that begins, "And now, you rich people, listen to me! Weep and wail over the miseries that are coming upon you . . . you have not paid any wages to those who work in your fields. Listen to their complaints" (NRSV). Later, at a lunch meeting the minister told me that there is just too much pressure on him to question anything in the world of business since the congregation is largely made up of businessmen.

Hong Kong ministers could be best described as managers since they spend most of their time managing the church enterprise, says Kwok Nai-wang. Church leaders are praised when they display traits and values appreciated in the marketplace. Prior to 1997 many church groups were busy with managing their properties and speculating on values post-1997. The Southern Baptists recently sold some properties that earned them HK$400 million. The Episcopalians also just sold a piece a property that went for HK$300 million. One large evangelical group told me that they sold almost all of their properties because they feared a drop in the property market. This church has been able to pay for all of its property rental fees off the investments. The Methodist Church of Hong Kong managed to change the "land use" designation of their property grant in order to do property development. The traditional architectural styled Methodist church of Wanchai was torn down and replaced with a much taller "business" tower. The bottom thirteen floors are claimed for church use while the top ten floors are rented out to local businesses for church profit. They are able to receive premium rental income because of their location. The local church praises this move as "savvy."

These savvy calculating business decisions embody the values cherished in Li Ka-shing. One local described it this way, "Christians in Hong Kong are mostly professionals, middle, and upper class. Hong Kong people are also very pragmatic. So they see no problem with utilizing their accountants and professional resources within the church to make it grow and develop economically. Hong Kong values are the values of the middle class. So the church has no problem swinging a deal to gain more property or financially better its situation. The Methodist Church on Hennessy road is viewed pragmatically."

The Anglican Church was "too successful" according to several important church leaders. Anglican Bishop Peter Kwong sold church land to Cheung Kong Properties, owned by Li Ka-shing. The land, located near the Chinese University of Hong Kong, was converted from an orphanage into a private housing development. The Anglicans made millions of dollars. I was told, "Kwong grabbed the money and claimed a victory for the church, but the plan backfired." Tithing dropped to sixty thousand per year, down from 35–36 million per year. In 1999, Bishop Kwong tried to raise two million dollars but could not do it.

The Hong Kong Chinese Christian Churches Union (HKCCCU) has 240 million dollars in cash reserve. A minister of a large Chinese church refuses to join. "They only want the rich people to join. They receive 2 percent of the total tithe from each church. Rhenish Bishop Li Chee-Kong has created a multi-million dollar club." A spokesperson for the HKCCCU told me proudly, "The Union has become very strong financially. We manage several properties that we earn rental income from. We have some good financial managers who have done well with investments with our money."

Locally, church organizations and Christian individuals have amassed a vast amount of material resources. But beyond these local interests, since the opening of China's borders, Hong Kong churches' interests have moved to China along with business interests. Silence on controversial issues and cooperation within the social structures of power prove the best way to keep the borders open to these interests. Hong Kong, though, from its inception as a colony was viewed as a "stepping stone" to China. Many describe China as a "mission field ripe for harvest." Especially among evangelical organizations, which measure success by the number of converts, China is viewed pragmatically as the best place to concentrate resources. With communism demonized as an enemy, evangelical organizations raise millions of dollars in the West for programs to "penetrate China." A local pastor laughs at these efforts saying, "If you want to change a communist, just take them to the USA and let them see the supermarkets and Las Vegas. There is no hope for communism once they see this." I discuss later the importance of these flows between Mainland China and Hong Kong for the structuring of social relations.

One of the largest controversies in Hong Kong since the handover is over the "right-of-abode" of children of Hong Kong citizens born in Mainland China. On January 29, 1999, the Court of Final Appeal (CFA, the highest court in Hong Kong) ruled that all Chinese citizens who are children of Hong Kong permanent residents born outside of Hong Kong have the right of abode in the Hong Kong Special Administrative Region (HKSAR), irrespective of whether their parents had became a permanent resident at the time of their birth. But at the request of Chief Executive Tung Chee-hwa, the Standing Committee of the National People's Congress (NPC) in Beijing on June 26, 1999, reinterpreted Articles 22 and 24 of the Basic Law to effectively overturn the Hong Kong CFA's decision of Jan. 29, thus retrospectively denying the right of abode in Hong Kong to thousands of people from mainland China. This has been a high profile incident that brings into question the meaning and reality of "one country, two systems."

This decision has already created a great deal of hardship by separating families according to the Asian Human Rights Commission. Thousands of persons still face deportation to Mainland China from Hong Kong. I raise this issue because a small number of Christian social activists became involved defending the rights of these children to remain with their families. One Christian group, the Hong Kong Women's Christian Council, who has opposed the local Government and Beijing to fight for the rights of these displaced children, was notified by the Inland Revenue Department that its activities might not be compatible with its charity status (Hon 2001). The group replied that one of its aims is to fight for social justice. A second warning was sent citing cases in the United Kingdom that some organizations practicing similar "political" activities have been ruled non-charitable and therefore lost their tax-exempt status.

The kind of theological discourse and practice represented by this organization is highly unusual for Hong Kong Christians. The majority of Hong Kong Christian organizations support the system even in silence. They have good economic reasons to do so. As of July 26, 1991, there were more than seven thousand non-profit organizations listed on the Hong Kong government's "List of Approved Charitable Institutions and Trusts of a Public Character" which awards them tax exemption. Churches operate 80 percent of these non-profit organizations (Mak 1991, 13).

As pointed out in the "Descriptive Integration" chapter, Christian institutions control a large amount of local resources and receive many privileges. Silence and cooperation seem to be the current strategy for retaining their place in the social structure. "This is the mentality of the institutional church . . . because they have built up an empire, not with the church's money, but with someone else's, the government. There are a lot of jobs on the line. They don't want to give them up," says Kwok Nai-wang. The church is the second largest employer in Hong Kong after the government.

The above example is just one case of how Christianity, practiced at the margins of the structural power, is receiving pressure from Beijing and local government to support and represent business interests. But there are others, including pressures from within the church. Several ministers acting as social activists were pressured to consider a leave of absence. Internal conflicts of interest in the Hong Kong Christian Council (HKCC) precipitated a major turnover of staff including the resignation of general secretary Kwok Nai-wang. Kwok, frustrated that the HKCC had effectively been co-opted by the "unholy alliance" through the top leadership in the Protestant church, founded the Hong Kong Christian Institute to exercise a "prophetic role" in society. Outspoken staff on the Public Policy committee of the HKCC, which was originally created to monitor policy issues in Hong Kong in light of social injustices, were replaced. The problem of the church in Hong Kong, according to Kwok, is its dependency that has grown out of the colonial relationship between the church, the government, and the business elites. Dependency means simply "you side with the powerful." The dominant concern for institutional survival creates a silence. "You are not able to criticize the injustice which the government and the business tycoons, the powerful people, have created." Kwok challenges the church community "to de-link with the power structure in order to criticize the power structure."

One leading social activist who was an early advocate for social justice in the 1970s did take a study leave to England in order to "clean up his activist record," as he tells me. At this same interview his friend, a local pastor, teased him saying, "Look at him now. He is quiet about social activism, and he is happy driving his Mercedes that is parked out in the parking lot. If you want success and if you want church growth, don't follow the social movements. Church growth means you can make more money and drive a Mercedes and enjoy life." This pastor continued saying the elders in his church have warned him not to get involved concerning politically sensitive issues: "Don't stick your head out."

During a visit in June 1996 from the Religious Affairs Bureau (RAB), an arm of the Chinese Communist Party (CCP), Ye Xiao-en, director of the RAB, asked one thing from Christians in Hong Kong: "All we want is your respect and your patriotic devotion to your country" (Ye 1996, 10). A number of letters and articles quickly followed questioning the meaning behind "patriotic devotion." Patriotism for people in Hong Kong means something different from those living in the People's Republic of China. Deng Zhao-ming, former director of the Christian Study Centre on Chinese Religion and Culture (CSCCRC), says: "People in China define patriotism as 'following the party' whereas people in Hong Kong would define it as 'love of country.' This is a very important distinction." A local theologian explained to me, "We may love the mountains, the scenery, the cheap food, but in terms of the government we have a lot of hesitation." Another church leader said he has no problem calling himself Chinese. "But I do have a problem swearing my allegiance to the CCP. In other words, I love China, but it does not mean that I love the ruling party. And you cannot say that I am not patriotic. I identify with the people, the land, but not necessarily the government." What Ye Xiao-en appears to mean by patriotic devotion is to leave politics to your new sovereignty and keep faith in its proper social domain, religion.

A similar controversy occurred nine years earlier when Ye's colleague warned that it was "necessary to define the borderline between religion and politics . . . that Christianity exceeded the boundaries of religious activities when developing a political force" (San 1987). Anglican Bishop Peter Kwong agrees arguing, "The church should not be involved in politics. Instead it should nurture people to be more mature, thus enabling them to face any political situation" (Lau 1987, 24). He warned his clergy "to get his approval before becoming involved in non-church activities." Again, it appears that the leadership of the church in Hong Kong believes it is important to restrict the role of Christianity to private belief and the "religious" social domain.

But this presents a number of problems right from the start, say a number of theologians, when, in Chinese, the idea of "separation of church and state" is translated as "separation of religion and politics" (Kuang 1993; Lo 1997). In Chinese, the word for church (*gau wui*) and the word for religion (*jung gau*) share a similar character (*gau*). Along the same lines, the Chinese word for government (*jing fu*) and the word for politics (*jing jee*), share the same first character (*jing*). There is confusion often over the meaning of these social domains in translation when compared to western theological constructs of separation of Church and State. Joseph Kuang wants to see the whole western theological construct go with the colonial administration. The Christian community hears his voice but they are not concerned. It is not that they disagree. The majority of Christians are simply not interested in the debate.

A local church leader suggested that the Catholic Church provides a barometer for what is happening with churches at large in Hong Kong. Locally, one observes the silence of Cardinal Wu on all political issues since discussions began between Britain and China in the early 1980s. In contrast, Catholic Bishop Joseph Zen has become an outspoken advocate for social justice raising concerns for both China and the local Church. I spoke with Bishop Zen to get his perspective on Christianity in Hong Kong. His story is telling.

At the end of the 1980s there was talk of electing an appropriate bishop to succeed Cardinal John Wu when he retired after 1997. A bishop generally retires at age seventy-five. There was no consensus at the talks for a successor. The nuncio began looking around and finally chose Joseph Zen. "Zen who?" was the common response. Zen was largely unknown in Hong Kong. He was born in China and was educated and worked in Shanghai up until 1949 when he was forced to leave. He was a Salesian, an order known for their work amongst the poorest of the poor. In the early 1980s, the Catholic Church in Hong Kong like most churches in Hong Kong began focusing on reestablishing ties with China and reopening churches within China. Zen was appointed to this work because of his familiarity with China. He traveled circuits within China teaching and meeting priests for most of the 1980s and 1990s. A local priest, Father Naylor, surmises that Zen was chosen because he knew China well and more importantly China accepted and trusted Zen. He may not have been high on the "power list" in Hong Kong, but the political situation of 1997 called for a different set of criteria for the bishop. He was thus conferred with the official status of the right for succession of Cardinal John Wu.

The trouble began when Zen began to speak out for social justice on behalf of the poor and oppressed. This makes sense when one considers his theological commitments within his Salesian tradition. But his theological commitments clash with the commitments of Cardinal Wu, the established Church, and Chinese authorities. Zen is now a central figure in Hong Kong in the fight for the rights of new immigrants from China. This creates friction both with China and with the local government. He helped open five new primary schools for new immigrant children, who are perceived locally as "dirty and backward." This has not made him popular among local Catholic leaders. Catholic schools are known for their prestigious status in Hong Kong. He speaks against human rights abuses in China. This does not make him popular with Beijing. He has not been allowed to visit China since November 1998. In November of 1998 he met with a senior Religious Affairs Bureau (RAB) official who said we just do not feel secure letting you come in. In 1999 he was denied a visit again. When on January 6, 2000, there was the ordination of several Chinese priests in Beijing, he was not allowed to visit. He made a brief phone call to Beijing that revealed bluntly, "Beijing was very displeased with me." Finally, when Cardinal Wu submitted a letter to Rome in 1999 requesting to retire, his request was denied. Catholic leaders in Hong Kong also express concern over Zen becoming the next Cardinal, as this would mean possibly more trouble with China. They support Cardinal Wu's silence on controversial issues.

Bishop Zen shared his perspective on the controversy surrounding the canonization of 120 martyrs from China on October 1, 2000. This example illustrates the ongoing power struggles between the transnational Catholic Church, the mainland Chinese state, and Hong Kong people. It questions the intent and meaning of Hong Kong's "one country, two systems." Relations of power shape history, identity, and how faith is embodied in local practice and discourse. The martyrs were canonized on October 1, China's National day. The date became the first problem. Rome claims it did not realize it and that the canonization had no political implications as it was also the day of feast of St. Theresa (an appropriate date). Beijing refused to allow the Catholic Church in China to celebrate the canonization because the 120 martyrs were all considered imperialists, lawbreakers, and deserving of death. Beijing through unofficial channels asked the Hong Kong Catholic Church to celebrate quietly. The Hong Kong Church complied, but Bishop Zen asked, "What does this mean?" He immediately submitted his disapproval of the way China was handling the canonization in a local paper. To make things more interesting, it was the Taiwanese Catholic Church that was instrumental in researching and choosing the 120 martyrs. These martyrs are people they knew. History cannot be read as neutral, and further, religious history cannot be read apart from political history. When asked about the role of the church in Hong Kong with regard to China, Zen says, "This is a matter of deciding between standing for objective truths or choosing practical convenience. The church has opted for convenience. Someone must tell the world what is happening in China. The things that are happening go against the basic nature of the Catholic Church. This is why I recently published my article quickly in the Ming Pao instead of the weekly Sunday examiner. When a few Catholic priests made their statements against Rome on the canonization matter, I had to speak out." The Catholic Church, like the mainline Protestant church, holds a privileged position in Hong Kong, and they do not want to lose it.

The evangelical churches in Hong Kong have taken a slightly different approach but one that ends with self-censorship on China or political matters. Evangelicals have theologically made politics irrelevant to their faith. What matters is personal "spirituality" and individual "salvation." Further, they have a great interest in evangelizing China and any involvement in politics may draw unwanted attention to their group that might impede access to Mainland China. They offer resistance but only covertly. They are active in illegal proselytizing, Bible smuggling, and connecting with the unregistered house church groups.

Many of the local church leaders, when asked about connections with China churches, cautiously admit they have mission work in China but that this activity is not publicized even among their own constituents. One pastor said, "We have no energy for politics." Another said, "The quiet survive in China." Many shared that if they just keep a low profile, they could continue their work in China. Maintaining a low profile amounts to keeping quiet about China and politics. One Christian leader in Hong Kong says that, "tactically speaking, the church has changed its position in order to bolster its own position. The politically correct position has been to support the TSPM churches." He went on to explain that from the 1960s to the 1980s most Hong Kong Christians supported the underground churches and were anti-Three Self. Now, "their theology has gone northward to Nanjing, headquarters for the TSPM and CCC. With the political changes and issues of power tied to the handover, most Christian leaders have suddenly become pro-TSPM." One older church leader said that "the churches in Hong Kong use to regularly have hot debates on who to side with: TSPM or house church." But now, since the 1997 issue arose and China has opened its doors, the division is no longer as clear, and the public debates are no longer as important. Regardless of the disappearance of public debates on the issue, I still found strong opinions. The more evangelical Christians I spoke with clearly sided still with the underground church. It was a theological issue for them. Many felt strongly that the TSPM churches were not biblically sound, or some even more strongly felt that they were not of God. Often I heard the stories of personal suffering at the hands of TSPM church leadership. One pastor shared that church leaders simply won't discuss openly their China work because "we don't want to annoy Hong Kong people who suffered under the communists."

For different reasons, the majority of all Hong Kong churches are apolitical. "Churches realize that they have a better chance of getting into China by supporting the TSPM. Superficially then, the Hong Kong church supports the TSPM. But Chinese people often say one thing and do another." This is true of all the mainline church leaders I spoke with. All openly supported the TSPM churches and thus were able to build relationships based on the "three mutuals: non-interference, mutual respect, and non-subordination" (Basic Law). A major church organization admits that they follow the "three mutuals," but because they have established trust, they "now have non-official channels to work in China" to conduct activities typically considered illegal.

One leader admitted that giving money goes a long way in establishing trust. Churches and Christians in Hong Kong give a great deal of money to Christians in China (Cheng 1998). Often large sums are donated particularly for rebuilding a former church destroyed during the Cultural Revolution. The HKCCCU have helped build four new seminaries in China with donations. Recently, a Hong Kong seminary was given permission to reclaim land it held in China before 1949 to build a new seminary (Chia 1999, 179). I was told many village cadres now embrace the rebuilding of local churches because money will follow for other projects through former lineage or denominational ties. Although denominational ties are said to have vanished, "people still remember." Many churches in China are rebuilt with funds from the foreign denomination that founded it. Once money is provided to rebuild a church, Chinese officials look the other way, and they are able to gain opportunities to openly preach, teach, and evangelize in the community.

CHRISTIANITY AND POWERLESSNESS IN HONG KONG

Kwan warns of a developing a pathology that "when the want of the market becomes too omnipotent that the need of the vulnerable is trespassed" (Kwan 1999, 370). Aihwa Ong asks "about the way being human is at stake in the novel intersections of these domains." Along with Hong Kong's material success has come a growing gap between the wealthy and the poor. At the same time, Hong Kong is both described as a capitalistic miracle and as one of the world's most unfair economies where just five families control 80 percent of the Hong Kong stock market (European Union, December 2000).

A study done in the year 2000 showed that one person in six in Hong Kong or 1.24 million people live below the poverty line earning less than HK$2,500 a month (Wong 2000, September 26). Yet the common perception in Hong Kong is that classes do not exist. Hong Kong Policy Views, a pressure group on social affairs, conducted a poll in September 2000 that showed the attitude of Hong Kong people created obstacles in tackling poverty amid a widening gulf between rich and poor (Wong 2000, October 7). The findings reflected the fact that Hong Kong people had little knowledge of poverty. "Most of them only blame individuals' faults as the origin of poverty, failing to look at the structural problem in society which gives rise to the problem," says the lead researcher.

Hong Kong people believe in the myth of capitalism that everyone has an equal opportunity for wealth if they just lived out the values and actions of Li Ka-shing (Lau 1988). During an interaction time with a group of Hong Kong seminary students, they told me, "We all have our story of poverty. We were all at one time poor. This is the story of Hong Kong. But now that our families have become wealthier, our feelings have changed. We are not poor anymore and do not want to be again." The church is largely professional, educated, and middle class. They have little sympathy for the poor because they have their own stories of poverty and they figured their own way out.

The churches' primary response to the poor has been an institutional response through church run social service programs. A local Christian social worker says, "When I go to church, they all say this work with the poor is your job. I cannot get them involved." I asked the leaders of a local denomination if and how their churches are responding to the issue and needs of the new immigrants from China, Hong Kong's new poor. They could only conceive of this as a "social work" response that required partnership with the government or alternatively greater church growth and internal financial giving for welfare handouts. In the end they communicated that they did not have the resources or energy to deal with the poor.

Another pastor shared, "Ministry to these kinds of people requires special programs and resources" and therefore our ministries target the middle class. Further, he said, the poor have very difficult work schedules that do not fit into our normal Sunday morning worship and weekly activities. Another local church leader said, "It is much easier to preach to the middle class because they are more likely to become good members. The poor are a burden. They need help. That is why we have focused on student evangelism. They are quick and easy converts (to Christianity)."

Christianity plays an important role in supporting the structural relations of power that privilege an economic elite in Hong Kong. The church community identifies with values of the middle and upper class. But at the margins of society and church there are Christian activists and ministers who challenge the political and economic arrangement of social relations that exclude the poor. In the next chapter, I introduce stories of theological resistance to show that Christianity is contested terrain. There are alternative ways of envisioning and embodying Christianity that challenge the social relations of power embodied in the practice of Christianity as an "unholy alliance."

5

Prophetic Imagination—
Theological Alternatives to Power

There is also concrete truth in the notion advanced by others that systems of religious belief and practice can be modes of resistance against conquerors and exploiters. What we have not yet done systematically is to look at the multiplicity of symbolic actions as ideology, as expressions of different interests and aspirations embodied in cultural forms.

—Eric Wolf, *The Vicissitudes of the Closed Corporate Peasant Community*

Signification and symbolic production is never conflict free.

—Eric Wolf, *Ideas and Power*

If religion is inevitably bound up with the naturalization of power and the legitimation or sanctification of the world it constructs or inherits, it also enables [and directs] meaningful agency.

—Michael Lambek, *The Anthropology of Religion and the Quarrel between Poetry and Philosophy*

INTRODUCTION

THIS CHAPTER INTRODUCES THE reader to Hong Kong Christianity envisioned as an alternative or resistance to the Christian discourse and practice described as an unholy alliance in chapter 3. These voices emerge most often but not always from parachurch organizations involved in mission to Hong Kong's grassroots people. Grassroots refers to a "class" of people who are economically, politically, and even theologically powerless. An organization may be considered parachurch when the leadership and organization is located outside the institutional church. The boundaries between parachurch and church organizations are certainly not clear. In fact, parachurch groups exist in part over contested theological meanings and the practice of Christianity. Some argue that their parachurch ministry was really the ministry of being church and therefore mislabeled. The voices chosen for this chapter represent those parachurch groups who contest the meaning and practice of Christianity by resisting the structural and organizational power of the dominant church and society especially over the meaning and place of the powerless in Hong Kong society. These Christians envision and embody Christian mission as largely one of crossing economic boundaries rather than the traditional view of crossing ethnic boundaries.

This chapter reveals that Christianity in Hong Kong is a contested social practice, and the struggles over ideas are integrally related to power. The resistance appears in two different ways. One is more consciously envisioned as resistance by speaking to the powerful directly through the overt condemnation of injustices. The other way, representing the larger group of resistance, envisions and embodies resistance by the way they relate to the powerless. What is common to this resistance is a critique of Christianity envisioned as a private, individualistic, spiritual, and otherworldly affair and an alternative Christianity proposed that crosses social domains, enters the public realm, and addresses the material world here and now. As one social scientist observes of one such group, "they envision radical political, economic and social changes here on earth, and the changes are expected to be instituted through supernatural forces" (Chan 1995, 67). They represent then a challenge to the structural relations of power in Hong Kong. Ideas are implicated as crucial to the maintenance of the flows and relationships of labor, commodities, and capital that make up the structural relations of power. How one envisions the world determines how fit one may be for "capitalism" as much as one may be fit for "Christianity." The maintenance of the structural relations of power requires a kind of discipleship both in political-economic terms as well as in theological terms. The voices and practices of Hong Kong Christians presented in this chapter could be called "unfit for Christianity" and "unfit for capitalism." In many cases I actually heard this said.

SHEPHERD COMMUNITY CHURCH NETWORK

Ben Wang currently works as a pastor and director of a local grassroots cell church network, Shepherd Community Center. Ben is very different from your typical Hong Kong pastor. The first time I met him, he was wearing faded blue jeans and a brightly colored sweatshirt. With his long hair and non-professional style, one might first guess he sold illegal CDs as a member of a local gang or possibly he was one the latest Cantonese pop stars. His dress and colloquial Cantonese gave away whom he wanted to identify with and that it would not be with the majority of Hong Kong church members and definitely not their leaders.

He finished a master of divinity degree in 1982 at China Graduate School of Theology, a local seminary known for its early commitment to local Chinese leadership. After graduation, he worked as a pastor at what he called a typical local church. He would have remained in this traditional track of ministry if not for an experience in 1984 when he "discovered that he lived in a city" when he attended a seminar by a visiting urban missiologist, Ray Bakke. Ray lectured on urban life, and gave an assignment to them to walk in the district around their churches with a new set of questions and methods of observation. Ben said with a laugh, "that experience ruined my ministry." "I had always walked through my neighborhood. This was the first time I had ever walked in my neighborhood."

His church was located in Kwun Tong, an important manufacturing district. He realized that the people who lived and worked in this district were not the people who came to his church. Furthermore, he realized that even if they did come to his church, they would feel out of place. He began to see that, for the most part, Hong Kong church life was an upper middle class phenomenon. He decided in order to reach these people he would have to change the "idea of church . . . the foreign language, songs, sermons, and even time of meeting." Church was traditionally about the "holy hour called worship" on Sunday mornings when many restaurant workers, bus drivers, and workers were busy, so he decided to make church about Monday through Saturday.

These changes eventually led to conflict with the leadership who were still the professional middle class and Ben was asked to resign. He and a colleague, Tony Chan, eventually founded Shepherd Community Church in 1987, a "church among the grassroots people." Before they began, Tony took a job as a factory worker for six months in order to learn and better identify with the life of grassroots people. Without any guarantee of salaries, they proceeded to live and minister among the grassroots. They continue to this day to work without a guarantee of a weekly income having decided that it is important "to do ministry on faith." Shepherd Community Grace Church creates community for factory workers and marginal youth. He says that about 80 percent of the church members are grassroots people.

The Shepherd Community Fuk Lam (Temple Street) Church, started by Sam Lai in 1989, works to rehabilitate prostitutes and drug addicts. Sam Lai also does not typify your local pastor. He was a policeman for over twenty years working in the very neighborhood that he now pastors, Yau Ma Tei. But he admits that he was corrupt, using his work as front for crime as well as his own heroin addiction. He had been a heroin addict for twelve years before he met Jackie Pullinger, a British missionary who founded St. Stephen's society, a very successful drug rehabilitation program. Her program was recognized by China prior to the handover as a model social services agency that should not fear being disassembled. He spent a year in recovery, and then, drug free, he decided to return to his old neighborhood to plant a church among the people that he saw neglected by most churches and society.

The church owns a second floor space for meetings just a half a block north of the famous Tin Hau Temple which the street is named after. But most of their time is spent on the streets especially at night caring for prostitutes and drug addicts. It is not uncommon to find Sam and his congregation conducting a worship event at the night market on Friday nights and then spending the evening socializing with the crowds. Temple Street turns into Hong Kong's largest outdoor market every night after 6:00 p.m., running from Jordan Avenue to the Yau Ma Tei MTR (mass transit railway) station. By 8:00 p.m., Temple Street becomes a bustling frenzy of entertainment, eating, and shopping. One can find cheap clothes, electronic gadgets, illegal music and movies, fake watches, and a bowl of noodles. You can also find Chinese opera singers, fortune-tellers, and young women standing behind stalls advertising their services to the passing male clientele.

On one evening that I visited Sam and his church, I took with me two young seminary students who grew up in Hong Kong but nevertheless said this was an entirely new experience. They spent much of the evening with other members of Shepherd Community Church socializing with the older men near the temple who were gambling for HK$10 over a game of Chinese chess. They interviewed a Nepalese hawker who they learned had only come to Hong Kong four years ago to make enough money to support his family back home. They spent some time with a young prostitute who would be going home that night with some of the female church workers. Later, they shared that the evening's experience raised many questions for them.

Both came from churches that were predominantly middle and upper class. One came from Hong Kong's second largest church (over 3500 members) whose membership greatly expanded since Hong Kong emigrants returned in large numbers back to Hong Kong, most with college degrees and holding professional jobs. They said these people would never be accepted within their local churches let alone ever spoken to on the streets. One shared with Sam that his church now posts someone at the back of the church to escort back outside any street people because members were complaining about the smell. Several wealthier members threatened to move their membership and money if the problem was not taken care of. In sharp contrast, Sam counsels his members to always particularly welcome these same street people into their community. The vision of these churches is to "break down the four walls and to take the church to the people and to have a church that will suit all different types of people in the community."

JUBILEE (HEI FOOK) GRASSROOTS MISSION

Jubilee, founded by Agnes Liu in 1997, provides theological training "for the poor to go work among the poor." Jubilee joins the ranks of a growing number of theological training institutions and seminaries, bringing the total number in Hong Kong to twenty-seven. Jubilee stands out though from this growth of seminary institutions as Liu suggests it offers a critique of Hong Kong's existing seminaries. The story behind Jubilee is important for understanding the contested theological flows and power in Hong Kong.

Before founding Jubilee, Liu worked at Jifu, a similar theological program for the poor at the China Graduate School of Theology (CGST). Jifu translates as, "theological training for ministry among the basic stratum (lower class)" (Chang 1986, 365). Jifu refers to the "working class" or "blue-collar worker," but it also includes marginal youth, senior citizens, prisoners, drug addicts, squatters, and new China immigrants. The

Prophetic Imagination—Theological Alternatives to Power 87

Jifu program began in 1980 as a response to the "trend to capture the well-educated for Christian service" where the "theological schools focus their attention on the winners in the school system" (Chang 1986, 366). Jifu came as an indictment on the middle class values of the church, "which in turn reflects the value and structure of the society . . . The school system is part and parcel of the power structure . . . an oppressive system, maintaining the world view of the ruling group" (1986, 366–67). Jifu struggled to find support among local churches and even among faculty and students of CGST. One important theological educator in Hong Kong told me that soon after Liu left in 1996, the Jifu program closed down, according to one local theologian, because "the president and young scholars did not want Jifu there. CGST began thinking that Jifu brought down their academic image."

Agnes Liu embodies this marginalized image in a number of ways. I was told on a number of occasions that Liu was not recognized as an important theologian in Hong Kong for "she doesn't play the academic game. She doesn't do theology like the others from North America or Europe, like Carver Yu (CGST president) who is a Barthian. You must write Barth's theology to be accepted by Hong Kong. This theology is abstract, remote, and makes little sense to the everyday Hong Konger. This is the game theologians play. Liu doesn't play this game nor does she care to play this game." Liu replied to these criticisms by saying, "Christian leaders in Hong Kong have missed it on two points. One, their theology is foreign. They are unable to theologically address Hong Kong needs. Two, they neglect the poor." She continued, "Theologians in Hong Kong would rather debate postmodernism" than address the issues facing the grassroots people of Hong Kong like *bo mong ah* (dead visiting you), dreams, and *bo yung bo sah* (reciprocity). This reply can be validated in part by simply examining the content of local religious journals. Topics and footnotes all largely take up discussions and concerns that originate in the West. Agnes said, "Their theology and biblical studies are very contextual, but wrong context. They presume to participate in and teach from a universal theological position. But their position originates and deals with a western context."

She is marginalized further because of her degree. Hong Kong theologians do not accept the DMin degree. They see the PhD as the ticket of certification. Hong Kong is also very concerned about where you got that degree. Fuller Seminary in Pasadena, California, where Liu received her DMin degree, does not compare with Yale, Harvard, or Oxford. Liu also felt she needed a different degree but for different reasons. She studied under Paul Hiebert and Charles Kraft, two important missiological anthropologists. But she says, "I've used them all up. They do not help me move forward in Hong Kong." Liu finished a PhD in anthropology at the CUHK in 1999 studying a marginalized Hoklo settlement in the New Territories. "But her PhD is local (CUHK) and this is viewed poorly," another local theologian told me. "We have a saying in Hong Kong, 'the local *jinge* (cooking) is no good.'"

Finally, Liu along with other "charismatics" are viewed as suspect at best by many church leaders. She calls herself "spirit-filled" and believes those church leaders who ostracize them are "afraid of losing power when you talk about the Holy Spirit because you can't control the Holy Spirit." One pastor I interviewed reported that CGST let Liu go from Jifu largely because of her "radical thinking, encouraging faith healing, casting out spirits, and belief in the power of the Holy Spirit." There is a strong bias against "charismatics" among churches in Hong Kong. This is interesting in light of the tremendous growth worldwide of charismatic churches particular among the poor and grassroots. Where the majority of churches in Hong Kong are experiencing slowed to negative growth, independent churches associated with the charismatic movement are growing rapidly and especially among the grassroots people.

Why train the poor to minister to the poor? Liu provides several reasons. First, "Our Lord's words and deeds become our model to follow. Not only did he identify with the poor, he allowed them to have important roles in his kingdom" (Liu 1996, 279). Her biblical hermeneutic places a concern for the poor at the center of Jubilee's discourse and practice of Christianity. Secondly, examining the Hong Kong church through this hermeneutical perspective, Liu identifies a "theological problem" that Jubilee works towards solving. "The Hong Kong church needs to be delivered from its middle class captivity in order to be an authentic church of Jesus Christ. This deliverance must come about through structural redress of the current situation" (1996, 279).

This is a serious challenge to Hong Kong churches as well as to Hong Kong's twenty-seven other seminaries as she locates the problem of middle class captivity within the "power structure of the church" claiming that "the church will be evaluated vis-à-vis how she treats the naked, hungry, thirsty, sick, imprisoned and sojourning (Matthew 25:31–46)"

(1996, 280). This strong challenge, from her interpretation of Matthew, is a judgment on the path of Christians to either heaven or hell.

Quoting from Raymond Fung, Liu says the root of this theological problem is "the middle class domination of the world church whereby the middle class claims and exercises total power over the church and deprives all others of the openness to participate" (Fung 1989, 25). A survey of grassroots Christians in Hong Kong shows that "only 2.3 percent of them have group life in the church and only 2.5 percent of them serve as a lay person," placing the poor at the margins of church life and work (Liu 1996, 280). "Jubilee is about communicating the good news to the poor and building up a people of power among the poor." Liu believes that one of the best ways to empower the poor is to place them in control of their own theological discourse and practice of Christianity. The organizational structure of the church is such that those in power, the educated professional middle-class, perpetuate the structure of power they represent. At another level, what she calls cultural domination, the middle class captivity of the church remains because the values of Hong Kong's middle-class are the "norm to which they aspire" (1996, 280). Christian formation is at the same time the formation of middle class and neo-liberal worldview and values.

Liu tells a story of a local church that would be a common story for many of Hong Kong's churches. The church is located in an industrial area that in the beginning was a church largely of grassroots people. Now that they have largely all become middle class people, they have decided to move out of the neighborhood and change their mission focus. They told Liu that they no longer relate to the grassroots people. I heard this story often. "We all have our stories of poverty. It is a part of our experience that we no longer want to deal with. We've changed," says a group of local pastors. "Hence most of the poor that stay demonstrate a strong allegiance to the church but a weak allegiance to social class. They no longer feel a sense of responsibility and mission to the poor" (Liu 1996, 235). Liu concludes of the middle class captivity of the church: "structural grievances require structural redress" (1996, 280). Jubilee training center works towards addressing this structural grievance by providing alternative seminary education and placing the poor themselves in power of their own theological discourse and practice.

The training differs from other seminary education in a number of important ways. Jubilee's students are from among the working class and most who have not finished high school education. Their life experiences are valued as important over against formal systemized theological information. The learning process is informal, participatory, and student centered over against information centered formal classroom learning.

Agnes Liu shared with me a description of the "culture" and needs of grassroots people in Hong Kong. She understands culture to be an "integrated whole that when one subsystem of the culture (religious allegiance) changes, the other subsystems of the culture (social) must also change" (1996, 238). Therefore, she says, the greatest theological problem in mission concerns the "relationship between gospel and context." The context and "packaging of the message" are as important as the content. She begins with the presupposition that "conversion to Christ and incorporation into a church are two sides of the same coin" (1996, 238). Too often, conversion to Christ becomes conversion to middle class values and lifestyle because this is the dominant culture of the church in Hong Kong. "They are unable to differentiate between what is culture and what is Christian. Associating more with middle class Christians, they feel inferior and begin attending evening school, often at great psychological and social cost" (1996, 235). The problem with cross-cultural mission in Hong Kong is the "wide gap between church culture and grassroots culture." Christianity is problematically perceived to be:

1. ***Irrelevant to their lives.*** They are concerned about this life. The church talks about the next life. Christianity answers questions which they do not ask and it is silent on questions which they expect vital religion to answer.

2. ***Burdensome.*** (going to church every week, giving money, forfeiting the pleasures of life such as smoking, drinking, and gambling, the main rewards of their labor)

3. ***Very boring and dull.*** They do not want to sit through long sermons after they work forty-nine hours a week. Going to church is not their idea of rest.

4. ***Culturally distant.*** Most of the programs of the church are aimed at students and the middle class. The topics discussed are above their heads (science and faith, faith and history, Christological options and so on). English and intellectual jargon are used (Liu 1996, 233).

She points out that most grassroots people "think Christianity is a foreign and western religion." Christian religion from a "western" worldview is "abstract, concerned with a high god, about eternal life, ethics, and a message about sin understood as a transgression of some norms outside of their value system." But the grassroots people are interested in "the concrete, the world of spirits, how to have a good life now and solve real life problems (pragmatic), and understand sin as broken social relationships." Christian mission that operates out of the former context cannot "satisfy the needs of grassroots people." The primary needs of the grassroots people are economic including healthcare, education, and careers. These needs go unmet as long as mission focuses on an abstract notion of sin, God, and eternal life. The boundaries between these worldviews are not this clear in reality as she notes that grassroots people are being shaped by westernization, urbanization as well as traditionalism (1996, 231). But there still remains a clear distinction between life in the Hong Kong church, characteristically "western middle class," and life among the Hong Kong grassroots, characteristically "traditional Chinese."

This is the missiological problem says Liu, "Where can we put them (grassroots people) into the church? For it is rare to find a place in a traditional church in Hong Kong." A local pastor, who reflects the view of many pastors I interviewed, shared, "In my congregation we all believe in ministry to grassroots but when we get down to it, the parents don't want their children around the grassroots people. They don't want the negative influence. What are we to do?" I heard many other similar experiences in other churches reflecting the congregational disdain of the embarrassing habits and dress of the grassroots. Liu concludes, "These observations only confirm that the problem with cross-cultural mission in Hong Kong lies with the middle class cultural captivity of the church."

MISSION TO NEW ARRIVALS

Li Kin-wah founded Mission to New Arrivals (MNA) in 1997. Li says, "It is about networking with Hong Kong churches to help the new arrivals." The new arrivals he refers to are the recent wave of immigrants from mainland China, most of whom are women and children seeking right-of-abode with their families living in Hong Kong. Li runs MNA as well as pastors a church in Shatin that embodies his vision of mission to new arrivals.

On one of my visits with Li, he shared the story of a new immigrant and his family he had just been visiting at a local hospital. The new immigrant had tried to commit suicide by jumping off a bridge just two days ago. He was angry that the media coverage had misrepresented the new immigrant and his family by giving them a negative image. The media focused on the new immigrant's "irrational act" and failed to communicate the hopelessness of his situation and the role society plays in shaping his disadvantages. "The media shapes our culture" by consistently portraying new immigrants in a negative light. Anthropologist Alan Smart shares a similar view that the general population in the 1990s has created an "invidious distinction" of new arrivals versus Hong Kong people (Smart 2001, 37). The new arrivals are perceived as backward, stupid, dirty, lazy, undeserving, and poor.

I made it a regular practice to ask about the perception of the new arrivals among Christian communities that I visited. A group of seminary students was asked, "What has been your experience with new immigrants?" The students one by one shared their experiences that confirmed what Li and Smart both observed of society, including the church. They all tend to view the new immigrants in a negative light. But none of the students had ever experienced any significant contact with a new immigrant at their work, at their church, or in their social life. "The reality is," said one student, "that our middle class church has difficulty accepting new immigrants and their way of life."

One of the goals of MNA, says Li, is to answer two questions for Hong Kong churches: "Why should we help the new immigrants" and "what is the relation between mission and culture?" The vision for MNA begins with God's command to take care of sojourners (hospitality) and more broadly to care for the poor. It is a command that spans both the Old and New Testaments. The church in Hong Kong has cared for refugees and immigrants in the past during two other significant migrations from mainland China during 1950s and then 1970s, and later also for Vietnamese refugees in the 1970s. Why has the church neglected the new immigrants of the 1990s? Before 1997, only about ten churches had ministries to the new immigrants. A 1999 survey of churches showed 64 percent of Hong Kong churches had "no concern" for new immigrants, 22 percent were "willing to add services," and 14 percent were "considering a start" (Li 1999, 206). Up until 1997 Li points out that the church primarily "focused on the political situation" to the neglect of "the life of people in Hong Kong." Through the efforts of MNA, there are now a few more than one hundred churches with ministries to new immigrants.

The government just released a statement that 150 thousand people are waiting in mainland China to come to Hong Kong to join their families (created by the mostly male immigrants of the early 1980s). The government allows for 150 immigrants with right-of-abode into Hong Kong daily. "We must ask now, what does 150 per day mean to us?" Li wants to pose this political economic question in theological terms. There are currently about two hundred thousand illegal immigrants in Hong Kong as well as eight hundred thousand legal new immigrants. Li asks, "What is the responsibility of Hong Kong churches" to the needs of these new immigrants?" "We in Hong Kong talk about going to China to evangelize but now they are coming to our door. Hong Kong people do not know the Mainland culture, but here is our opportunity to learn. So by serving the new immigrants, we are starting China ministry. But we are not ready to serve Chinese people. We just offer them money, but we do not participate with our whole self. We need to respond to their felt needs." When they do find their way into the church, "they do not want to go back to their own people." Li describes a conversion to a class consciousness that accompanies conversion to Christianity.

Consistent with Li's belief that mission begins with meeting felt needs, MNA offers assistance to concerns voiced by the new immigrant families. These include locating housing and furniture, tutoring children, language instruction (Cantonese & English), and job hunting. Learning Cantonese (and speaking it properly he emphasizes) is important to them for making friends and getting jobs. It is also the primary source and symbol of their felt discrimination. But their children are their primary concern for "the children are their hope for a better future." The children need tutoring not only in Cantonese but also in English. Li says, "I have been in ministry for over twenty years. I have seen many evangelicals complain that they do not get good responses from new immigrants. But they do not understand their felt needs. They speak based on their own need to share and convert."

The failure of mission to new immigrants, according to Li, is primarily due to prejudice and a failure to understand differences in culture. "Both sides have wrong concepts of each other. New immigrants think of Hong Kong people as rude and proud. Hong Kong locals think of new immigrants as backward and dirty." MNA's primary mission strategy is to create a "movement of the two groups toward each other." MNA works hard then to educate both sides to better understand real cultural differences. "We try to stir up the atmosphere by organizing fairs and inviting the media in order to create a better image of the new immigrants."

Li made a prediction for the future in Hong Kong and China as they relate to mission to new immigrants. Hong Kong pastors are conservative, slow to change, and not ready for new immigrant ministry. This is why MNA also works to support and equip pastors with resources they do not get from seminary education. We must act quickly for "my perception is that this ministry will only last ten years because the Mainland and Hong Kong will grow closer. There will be less attraction for Mainland people to come to Hong Kong. The next stage will be for Hong Kong people more and more to go to China. In five years, maybe, there will be Hong Kong communities in China that will need ministers."

INDUSTRIAL EVANGELICAL FELLOWSHIP

Industrial Evangelical Fellowship (IEF) grew out of a Christian student fellowship in 1973 at Hong Kong Polytechnic University. The organization has evolved over the years, but its mission remains the same, to serve the needs of the grassroots industrial workers. Poon Yu Miu-wan, the current general secretary, has provided leadership since 1994. She, along with her husband, worked as teachers at Jifu (forerunner to Jubilee) after they graduated from CGST. The need for specially trained theological workers for the grassroots and the support for the Jifu program at CGST grew out of the work at IEF. Agnes Liu Tat-fong (Jubilee) also worked for IEF in the early 1980s before going to Fuller seminary (California) for graduate study and then returning to Jifu. Among these parachurch organizations there is an important network of support in their common mission to the poor of Hong Kong. Li Kin-wah (MNA) also cooperates with IEF and the government in the development of their mission to aid new immigrants.

The context of IEF's development is important. By the late 1960s, Hong Kong had developed economically, considered by then as one of East Asia's "Four Little Dragons" or the "East Asian Tigers" (capitalist success stories including South Korea, Taiwan, Singapore, and Hong Kong). The church also grew with the economy and was by the early 1970s composed largely of middle class educated professionals (Karsen

1980, 30). Along with the tremendous economic growth came a widening of the gap between the rich and the poor. With the development of industry came a class of industrial workers who were open to exploitation. Because of the government's social non-interventionist policy, there were no laws or structures in place to protect the rights of the worker. The riots of 1966 and 1967, protests against the government's lack of concern for the local worker, came as an important critique of the social and theological development of Hong Kong as well as a response to the Cultural Revolution on the Mainland.

The church responded quickly to the government's call to reach out to the misunderstood youth. Youth for Christ, Campus Crusade, and the Fellowship of Evangelical Students organized groups along with many other independent youth Christian fellowships. But these efforts focused on the educated youth. The organization of parachurch institutions such as IEF and the Christian Industrial Committee (CIC) developed as advocates for the poor industrial workers. The churches of Hong Kong for the most part remained middle class and educated while these parachurch organizations began what has become the proliferation of groups from the margins for social, political, and economic justice.

The manufacturing population of Hong Kong reached its peak in 1971 at 47 percent (Salaff 1981, 18). A fairly steady flow of legal and illegal immigrants from the Mainland continued to supply cheap labor. The Hong Kong government recognized the problem of increasing rates of immigrants from the mainland as a result of the Cultural Revolution and officially reversed the open door policy in 1974. This second wave of immigrants (since 1949) came with no capital and no education. This new cheap labor force that had no unions or protection from the government's laisse-faire economic policies continued to draw a great flow of transnational capital from foreign investors. The gap between the rich and poor steadily grew.

It was in this context that a newly organized fellowship of Christian college students began to study their Bibles in light of their local contexts at the Chinese University of Hong Kong. One frustrated local theologian explained that this group of students in the 1970s became interested in social concerns through their study of the Old Testament prophets in Amos, Hosea, and Isaiah. They were social work majors. But when they began to speak in the church, the church discounted their views by declaring their perspective "social gospel and heretical." His frustration was highlighted by the fact that in 1974, when the Lausanne Covenant mentioned a few lines about social concerns, then suddenly it became acceptable because it came from the West. "These university students were so upset. They said what we work through in our own Bible study does not mean anything. But when a foreigner says in a few lines, John Stott says this or that, then it becomes permissible. The standard must be imported."

IEF's mission to the grassroots, which they define as workers engaged in physical labor, has its beginning in the Bible's concern for the worker. The mission of IEF identifies its mission with the mission of Jesus, using Luke 4:18 as the quintessential statement on Jesus' mission: "The Spirit of the Lord is upon me, because he has anointed me to bring good news to the poor." They view workers as the weaker group or as the sheep who are helpless without a shepherd (also using Matthew 9:36).

When I visited with Ho Ping-kwong, a staff member at IEF for twenty-one years, he shared his concern for the church in Hong Kong to theologically reflect on the current situation of Hong Kong's industrial workers. The manufacturing population declined to just 18.9 percent of the population by 1996 and that declining trend has continued as Hong Kong moves to more of a service and knowledge economy. When the Mainland opened in 1978, industry began its emigration from Hong Kong to China's cheaper labor source. According to government statistics, the manufacturing population in 1999 stands just below three hundred thousand people. This is a drop of 640 thousand people since 1986.

Ho says it is important for us to ask in theological terms what has happened to these people and how do they concern us as Christians. The majority of these people have no education beyond form five at the most and therefore are unable to transition into jobs in the new economy that require further education especially in science and technology. Some have been absorbed into catering (180 thousand), transportation (180 thousand), cleaning (forty thousand) or construction (eighty thousand). Some have returned to the mainland to obtain employment. But many are left unemployed, and those employed elsewhere receive minimal compensation. In the year 2000 alone, twenty thousand form five students will not pass the grade to advance and will be left unemployed. These are the poor grassroots workers with whom IEF concerns itself.

Prophetic Imagination—Theological Alternatives to Power   97

A common question Ho encounters when sharing with Hong Kong churches is "What is your priority, evangelism or social action?" The question is a common litmus test for many evangelicals to determine orthodoxy in Hong Kong. It is also a question born out of a different historical context in the early twentieth century America that was later transported through missionaries to Hong Kong. Ho responds, "No priority! Does there have to be one?" This is why many workers have "contradictory feelings" and are "suspect of Christian organization's thinking. The workers think they just want converts, but eventually IEF becomes their second home." The goal of IEF is simply to "meet the needs of the whole person and not press our faith on them." They need support with housing, economic concerns, interpersonal friendships, finding respect and trust, mediating factory disputes, and in addition their own spiritual concerns. "Our models for mission must change constantly to meet the changing needs of worker community." To do this we must know something about the "characteristics of the worker community."

Although reluctant to generalize about the "worker community," Ho has a list of general characteristics of the workers IEF ministers to. Ho makes the point that these characteristics are only a starting point. Understanding of each community will emerge more fully when those engaged in mission "fully participate in their life" and "build up good relations whether or not they become Christians." As a starting point, workers usually have low education levels, low and unstable incomes, limited economic security, and deal with low self-esteem as a result of perceived low social position. They are easily influenced by economic change in society and very pragmatic, that is, concerned about the present over the future. They initially view Christianity as a western foreign religion. They see church as only for educated people. Even if they thought they could fit in, they are not attracted to church perceived as dull, no fun, too abstract, and requiring too many restrictions. Whether or not they have any other religious beliefs, they are usually connected by way of parents to ancestor worship and so experience social pressures against Christianity. "Once a worker who becomes a Christian attends a church, they soon leave." IEF provides alternative worship and fellowship experiences outside the experience of the dominant Hong Kong church.

Responding to how IEF encounters support from Hong Kong churches and Christians, Ho says, "Before 1997 it was difficult, but now more are concerned about the workers. Grassroots people have become a prime concern after 1997." But the predominantly middle class churches still find difficulty incorporating workers. For instance, Ho says Gordon Siu, pastor of one of Hong Kong's largest churches (North Point Alliance), "gives great support to IEF by giving money, but that's it." North Point also has its own family support service to new arrivals, but Ho points out that these new arrivals are the wealthy professionals. "When you compare our family center with the Alliance family center you will notice they are very different. Their center is for their own wealthy family members. Ours is for the grassroots people."

HONG KONG CHRISTIAN INSTITUTE

The history of the Hong Kong Christian Institute (HKCI), organized in 1988 by Kwok Nai-wang, is especially important for understanding the direction of churches in Hong Kong. Kwok was general secretary of the Hong Kong Christian Council (HKCC) from 1978 to 1988. Prior to becoming general secretary, he was a pastor of Shum Oi Church, a unique attempt to include marginalized grassroots people in church and to be a voice for social justice in the community. He brought this theological perspective to the HKCC. When the 1997 issue arose, he moved his social justice perspective into the realm of politics to fight for democracy and human rights in Hong Kong as well as China. This move gradually came to dominate his leadership and vision for the HKCC. I was told that his support and direct involvement in 1986 of the protest against China's Daya Bay Nuclear Power project was what finally caused concern with other HKCC's committee members and church leaders. This story is one that no one I spoke with wanted his or her name attached to. But the story was consistently told as a power struggle between Kwok and Anglican Bishop Peter Kwong who wanted to move the HKCC and Hong Kong church toward establishing good relations with China. Kwok, on the other hand, represented a collision course with China. In 1988, Kwok resigned (under pressure), and organized, with 120 other church leaders, the Hong Kong Christian Institute (HKCI).

The HKCI organized "out of the sense of urgent need as well as frustration among Christians." Kwok continued, "If the churches themselves did not take the risk in taking a stand or getting involved in social and political action, perhaps a voluntary agency like HKCI could be formed alongside churches to help fill the need." Since 1988, there has been a clear split between the larger majority of churches that through cooperation and silence have worked to secure its position in the social structure after 1997 and HKCI's minority position over the political future of Hong Kong. Mainline churches cooperated in part by sending representatives to participate in committees to write the Basic Law (1989) and to select the first chief executive and preliminary legislative council. Evangelicals for the most part kept silent about changing political arrangements and focused on evangelism and internal problems.

At about the same time, and some from the impetus of the HCKI, other Christian activists groups emerged but remain marginal to mainstream Christianity. The Hong Kong Women's Christian Council (HKWCC) organized in 1988 to fight for the rights of women and the marginalized of society. The Hong Kong Christian Sentinels (1984) and Hong Kong Christian Democratic Patriotic Movement (1989) organized groups of Christian professionals to develop a more democratic system. In 1987, a group of recent university graduates organized the Christians for Hong Kong Society. One of its members said he joined just after the 1984 Joint Declaration was prepared. He said, "The formation of our faith was strongly influenced by this atmosphere. We developed a concern of the socio-political environment. When we graduated we thought we should do something to continue our ideals instead of only pursuing our careers. Then in 1989 the Democratic Movement in China aroused Hong Kong people and the Christian community. We were social activists, young and energetic at the time."

SUMMARY

This chapter provides examples of Christians and Christian organizations that contest the dominant practice of Christianity as an "unholy alliance." Their Christian discourse and more importantly practices offer a challenge and critique of social and material relationships naturalized and even sanctified by market, state, and church. Power manifests itself in relationships. Therefore, to advocate for the powerless and embrace the marginalized is to challenge the structural relations of powers and its flows—material and ideological. Certainly, I would not want these last two chapters to lead to the polarizing perspective that Christianity is embodied and envisioned as either complicity or resistance. The situation is much more complex. But these two broad perspectives are certainly pervasive and aptly describe how a Christian organization may or may not embody one or the other.

6

Conclusions

For awhile I have been saying how Hong Kong is "a one-issue town," to the incredulity of friends and associates who think the city is rife with problems jostling for attention. I reckon the noise sounding in every direction is really about one issue—that of power, who has it and who wants it.

—Peter Woo Kwong-ching, *Our One-Issue Town*

It is not just, I think, that symbols have a history and that they are used as instruments for some purposes. Symbol systems are constructed, by whom and for whom, by whom and against whom. I am trying to build up cases that will speak to these questions.

—Eric Wolf

Religion is both embodied and imagined.

—Roy Rappaport, *Ritual and Religion in the Making of Humanity*

OVERVIEW

THIS BOOK INTERWEAVES SEVERAL histories told from the vantage point of the handover of Hong Kong in 1997. I have tried to give a history of power and Christianity in Hong Kong, or in other words, a history of the interpenetration of capitalism and Christianity. These histories are surely limited in their scope, but I believe they do describe something real. I began by inquiring into the social processes of Christian identity making as a response to the unfolding historical processes of the perceived crisis of 1997. Hong Kong, a capitalist success story, faced the crisis of possibly losing its "capitalist system and life-style" as it returned to its new sovereign, socialist China. I demonstrated that the Christian response was a contested process closely intertwined with the broader contested processes of social organization in Hong Kong. I showed how Christianity came to Hong Kong along with the development of this capitalist way of life. What developed was a comprador Christianity that laid the foundation for what became embodied as an "unholy alliance," or better, a capital-friendly Christianity. But Christianity is not a fixed essence. I also showed how others envisioned Christianity differently as "prophetic imagination." How Christianity was envisioned is closely tied to how it was embodied in social and material relationships. I have presented a case study to develop our understanding of the political economy of formation—both Christian and capitalist.

CHRISTIANS—GOOD CITIZENS OR DANGEROUS DISSIDENTS?

China's perspective of Christianity enlightens the perspective I have offered here of Christianity in Hong Kong. In February 1998, a delegation of religious leaders from the United States made a three week trip to China with the express purpose to dialogue about religious freedom. The trip was organized by Bill Clinton on an invitation from Jiang Zemin. The issues that this trip hoped to address were the growing concerns of many members of Congress over religious freedoms and China's trade status as most favored nation (MFN). This story has implications for a discussion of power and ideas in the broader structural relations of power involving the United States, China, and transnational corporations and churches. But what I want to focus on is China's political economic understanding of Christianity.

Ye Xiaowen, director of China's Religious Affairs Bureau (RAB), views Christianity as a potential threat to the established ordered. Richard Cizik, policy analyst for the National Association of Evangelicals (NAE) and also one of the trip's members says: "They (China) don't understand the power of faith to change people's lives, the Christian teaching of the soul, or the Christian teaching of the conscience. They view [religion] through a political lens" (Mark 1998, 30). Cizik and other group members attempted to offer a defense of religious freedom and counter the belief among China's leaders that Chinese Christians pose a threat to the state by arguing that good Christians are good citizens and good workers. Rev. Don Argue, president of the NAE at the time and trip member, said, "We have stressed that people of faith are good citizens, honest people, who do their jobs and pay taxes. It's to China's advantage to work with such people... They serve in the military and they are volunteers in their communities" (Mufson 1998, A-21). Budde and Brimlow comment on this:

> One can perhaps forgive the dictators in Beijing for misunderstanding the political implications of Christianity. After all, in their internal dealings they have had to contend with an underground Catholic (and Protestant) Church whose members would sooner risk decades of imprisonment than subordinate the gospel to tyrants. The regime reads the New Testament and becomes uneasy; it becomes unnerving to read about the risen Lord leading people to step across the borders of nationality, class, and gender in the service of a Kingdom no government can control. The rulers of Beijing can be forgiven for their lack of experience with churches that join their religious and political loyalties, that are almost entirely at peace with militarism, economic exploitation, and national idolatry. (2000b, 4)

This story serves as an illustration of the primary issues this book addresses as well as their broader implications to the political-economic region in which Hong Kong is embedded. We move now to final conclusions.

POLITICAL ECONOMY OF FORMATION

One of the central theoretical concerns for this study has been the relationship of power to ideas, following closely the research agenda of Eric Wolf in *Envisioning Power* (1999). This study examines structural power and organizational power. Organizational power in Hong Kong is easy to identify at work because it is power that is immediately useful and practical. This is the instrumental power that exercises control over energy flows within the environment. It is the control of material and cultural resources and their associated rewards. It is this power that the majority of Hong Kong churches are afraid of losing for they have amassed a large reservoir of capital in its land, buildings, and people.

But this study is more interested in expanding our understanding of structural power. This is power that shapes the flow of energy from the outside that affects the possible fields of action. How ideas are implicated in these flows becomes an important question to this study because it also points to an important conclusion I reach. The structural relations of power are defined by more than just the flow of commodities, the accumulation of capital, or access to labor. There are also flows of values and ideas that serve to legitimize as well as challenge the making and unmaking of the structural relations of power. "Language and discourse are among the ultimate means of production" (Verdery 1991, 420). That is, the social relations produced by forces of capitalism depend upon ideational and formational processes. You could say that they depend upon being made "fit for capitalism" or incorporated into an ethos.

This research connects how being made "fit for capitalism" interweaves with being made "fit for Christianity." This helps us develop our understanding of structural power by connecting the material with the flow of values, ideas, dispositions, affections, and desires that in one way or another legitimizes or challenges the structural relations. Budde and Brimlow recognize this as they conclude, "Capitalism, no less than Christianity, depends on formation processes to sustain itself in the world; making people 'fit for capitalism' is no less important to the workings of the world economy than processes of production, distribution, and finance" (2000, 61). My goal, like Wolf, was not to develop a grand theory of power or "think of power as an all-embracing, unitary entelechy" (Wolf 1999, 66). Rather, it was in part to locate and explain power within social relationships and in particular within the social domain of religion.

This is how it has worked in Hong Kong—Christianity has been domesticated by becoming largely disembodied from public life. That is, the church has largely let capitalist values shape life by accepting that Christianity only speaks to the private, personal, and spiritual. What has developed is the apotheosis of money, markets, and commodities. Christian practice is largely envisioned and embodied as a retreat from the world by focusing on other worldly salvation and individual private spirituality. The formation of the Hong Kong subject is largely shaped by the values of neo-liberal capitalism that come with the naturalization and even sanctification of concepts as "free" market and laissez-faire economics.

But this is understandable. The organizational power of the church is directly related to how structural power operates. There is much to lose if Christianity were to challenge how relations of power are structured. Despite the risks, this is happening on the margins. Individuals and parachurch groups are challenging how social relations are structured by siding with the powerless and poor of Hong Kong. Because the very quality of power manifests itself in social relations, to advocate for the powerless or embrace the poor is to challenge the flows of power and stand against the social fields of structural power. My study, by examining the workings of structural power, developed an understanding of Christianity that goes beyond ecclesiastical hegemony to encompass struggles over human practice, meaning, and representation in relation to the changing political-economic context.

CHRISTIANITY AS PROPHETIC IMAGINATION

Signification and symbolic production is never conflict free.

—Eric Wolf, *Ideas and Power*

The unfalsifiable supported by the undeniable yields the unquestionable, which transforms the dubious, the arbitrary, and the conventional into the correct, the necessary, and the natural.

—Roy Rappaport, *Ritual and Religion*

Eric Wolf has been my guide for the course of this research, but I have journeyed on without him with the chapter on Christianity envisioned as "prophetic imagination." Wolf has focused on ideologies of dominance but has not offered much case study evidence of ideologies of liberation or hope. I certainly do not think this would be antithetical to what he has offered, and I find evidence that he points to where I have continued.

I continue with the help of Roy Rappaport (1999) and Michael Lambek (2000) who would agree that religion is often maladaptive and used as a force for domination but that it can also provide a significant source for adaptation, in particular, to the destructive "pseudo-religion of money and commodity consumption" (Rappaport 1999, 438–61). Wolf attempts to address this "problem of cosmology" by working with Rappaport's concept of "ultimate sacred propositions" and concludes that it is unlikely that they "remain in place by virtue of their own ineffable qualities" (1999, 285). Maybe Wolf just could not move from Marx who saw all religion as false to Durkheim who took all religion to be in some sense true.

Wolf would agree with Rappaport that by locating the sacred power at arms length from profane power enables it to sanctify it. But I agree with Rappaport that this same location of sacred power at arms length also enables it to curse profane power. This is the evidence I provide for in chapter 4. In one sense, everything that I explain through chapter 3 appears obvious, that religion is understood as a regime of power. What chapter 4 does is demonstrate what Lambek advocates for by drawing on Rappaport: "But what distinguishes the anthropology of religion from other fields of inquiry is that it cannot rest with power but must contextualize the very conception and production of power within a wider cultural order, one which will equally contain alternatives to power in its repertoire of ends and means" (Lambek 2000, 312).

Imagined worlds or ultimate sacred propositions can provide ideologies of liberation and hope for a better world. What is envisioned is certainly connected with what is embodied, but what is envisioned is not always domination. Wolf realized the insufficiency of power as a solitary or final explanatory principle. He agreed with his critics that everything cannot be reduced to power, and this is why he attempted such a project as *Envisioning Power*.

Chapter 4 provides evidence to explain desires, values, and commitments that are often antithetical to power. I wanted to account also for the force or power of love and justice. I have offered just a beginning here, as I will suggest along with Lambek a need for further research that considers the domain of morality alongside power and desire (2000). And I would note that it would be a mistake to limit a discussion of morality to the domain of the religious. If anything sums up this dissertation's perspective of Christianity in Hong Kong, I think it would be this conclusion reached by Lambek: "Religion at its best attempts to provide space and direction for moral practice, to enlarge opportunity and access; at its most limited, it aims to make a virtue out of the constraints. All this may be mystifying, but it is generally hopeful, and at least it moves people or, rather, gets people moving in some direction off the couch of habit and beyond the official discourses and the competitive search for symbolic and material capital" (Lambek 2000, 317).

THEOLOGY OF ASYMMETRIES AND INEQUALITIES

I don't consider myself to be a theoretician. My aim is not primarily to develop a theoretical framework . . . My primary interest is to explain something out there that impinges upon me, and I would sell my soul to the devil if I thought it would help.

—Eric Wolf, *An Interview with Eric Wolf*

> *We conceptualize power as a social relation built on asymmetrical distribution of resources and risks and locate power in the interactions among, and the processes that constitute, people, places, and resources.*
>
> —Susan Paulson et al., *Locating the Political in Political Ecology*

This may have been the place to start, and it is certainly the place to conclude this study of structural power and ideas. By focusing our attention on the inequitable distribution of resources within society, we can come to better understand the workings of structural and organizational power. An important conclusion of this research is to find power and ideas complicit in the formation and legitimization of inequality. This study would have been enhanced if I had focused the interviews and research on locating theologies of inequality instead of the broader concerns of the 1997 handover. What Christian discourse and practice have to say and do about poverty and powerlessness would have been a good guiding question for the research objective.

I think this research points to the need for those interested in development and underdevelopment to pay closer attention to the social domain of religion and theology. At the same time, the research points to the need of those engaged in the practice of religion to pay attention to how belief is embodied, particularly in harmful ways. The study of Christianity should not be placed at the margins of what anthropologists study. At the same time, anthropologists of religion need to move from any essentializing notions of religion to a more critical perspective that locates the "sacred" within the "profane," rather than distant to.

My goal was further to better understand the relationship of power to ideas in order to make a difference in the world. By necessity then, the study came to focus on the marginalized of society. Along with Wolf, I view anthropology as a "critical tool with which to address social concerns" that can be "used to create a better world" (2001, 2–8). This is why I began this study. Hong Kong continues to be reported positively by the world as the "freest economy in the world." Yet studies continue to show that the gap between the rich and poor continues to grow, rating seventeenth in the world list of greatest disparities between rich and poor (World Development Index 2002). Differences of power are embodied in social relations as well as envisioned in cultural configurations. Power depends upon our structured social memberships and locations as well as on our attendant capacities and willingness to mobilize culture to sustain a particular structured order over another.

LIMITATIONS OF THE STUDY

This does not mean that the attempt to insert power into our conceptual framework, and fuse it to culture, was misguided. To the contrary, it is a project whose time has come. Yet if a scholar of Wolf's stature ran into roadblocks, only an optimist would predict that anyone else will have an easier ride.

—Stanley Barrett et al., *The Idea of Power and the Power of Ideas*

I keep finding it all fascinating, even though "final" explanations elude me.

—Eric Wolf, *letter to Harald Prins in 1995*

The book (Envisioning Power) fell far short of my ambitions, but it stands as an expression of the central reason for being an anthropologist: to seek explanation for the world as I encountered it.

—Eric R. Wolf, *Pathways of Power*

Every study must accept certain limitations that come by taking a particular perspective and approach. I chose to take this research ride with Eric Wolf for the strength of his approach to explain the nexus of power and ideas in the making and unmaking of the world. The limitations of this approach have already been well documented. I am in danger of reducing everything to power, but I have avoided this by demonstrating that power is interdependent with ideas and social relations. This study avoids peddling a singular globalizing history of capitalism. Rather, it means to demonstrate the force of power mediated by local forms and people in the local context of Hong Kong.

The more significant limitation is the focus on structural power. But I chose this approach because I agree with Wolf, "There is too much talk about agency and resistance and too little attention to how groups mobilize, shape, and reshape cultural repertoires and are shaped by them in turn; how groups shape and reshape their self-images to elicit participation and commitment and are themselves shaped by these representations; how groups mobilize and deploy resources but do not do this 'just as they please'" (Wolf 1994, 6). I hope chapter 4 compensates for this potential loss of agency and resistance, by focusing on the structures that constrain human agency. I think this study could have benefited by incorporating a stronger picture of practice akin to the work of the Comaroffs and Burawoy.

Another strong limitation I faced while collecting data came with the sensitive nature of the research topic. Christian communities, particular church organizations, were hesitant to disclose information regarding politics or budgets. I feel the topic is of such importance that it is worth the risk of providing what can only be a partial and incomplete description. I am interested in how we as anthropologists could better study topics that are considered by our subjects and even ourselves as taboo, private, immoral, and even dangerous.

Finally, I faced certain limitations of access and methodology because of "studying up" or studying elites (Nader 1972). It was often difficult to gain access to people who had "lines of defense" or "gatekeepers" to protect their time and interests (Thomas 1995; Nader 1972). There was also difficulty utilizing participant observation, as I understood it as "designed for small, face-to-face societies." It is well noted that "participant observation is a research technique that does not travel well up the social structure" (Gusterson 1997, 115). Instead, I found myself most often involved in "polymorphous engagements"—"interacting with informants across a number of dispersed sites" utilizing an "eclectic mix of research techniques" (1997). The problem of studying seven million people is how to be both holistic and descriptive of the experience near. But I discovered that urban lives are lived in "small social worlds"—but also "where these spheres of lived experience are profoundly influenced by their location within the larger urban place and regional, national and global systems" (Smart 1999, 61).

RECOMMENDATIONS FOR FURTHER RESEARCH

I would argue that there is a crucial link, to be understood much better than we do now, between interest and morality.

—Eric Wolf, *The Vicissitudes of the Closed Corporate Peasant Community*

The recommendation to study morality alongside power and desire assumes a less fragmentary approach within anthropology. That is, anthropologists of religion need to avoid essentialized notions of religion to include a broader subject. Likewise, anthropologists who study politics and economics need to explore connections between the material and values and moral practice (Carrier 1997; Graeber 2001; Dilley 1992; Parry and Bloch 1989; Robbins and Akin 1999). We need a better way to theorize and explain values—monetized, materialized, and idealized. Graeber (2001) and Lambek (2000) in particular illuminate how we might begin this research.

IMPLICATIONS OF THE STUDY FOR MISSIOLOGICAL THEORY AND PRACTICE

We are thus more likely to be critics than architects of grand theory. This often assigns to us the unwelcome yet vital role of questioning the certainties of others, both social scientists and policymakers.

—Eric Wolf, *Anthropology among the Powers*

The way to the development of an Asian theology is not direct formulation of theological principles in an Asian way. I go further in suggesting that it is by way of commitment to the poor. The poor will help free us to build an authentic Asian agenda.

—Raymond Fung, *On Doing Theology in Asia*

The hardest lesson the church will have to learn in the coming years is how to become again what it originally was and was always suppose to be: the church without privileges, the church of the catacombs rather than the halls of fame and power and wealth.

—David Bosch, *Vision for Mission*

The argument for the place of anthropology in missiological research and practice precede my research project. But this study implies the need for expanded anthropological perspectives as well as anthropological roles. To start, there is a positive role to be played by the anthropological iconoclast. Concepts such as culture, theology, God, gospel, indigenous church, and contextualization among many others need to be continually reworked as tools rather than glorified as theoretical principles. Questioning certainties will certainly not endear one to the missiological community but it must be done. This perspective shares the conclusion that "what anthropology has to offer is a continuous questioning of the processes, assumptions, and agencies involved in development" (Gardner and Lewis 1996, 168).

In particular, this study would challenge missiologists to explore beyond the dominant "culturalist" anthropological theories and approaches. Efforts could be made to build upon culturalist perspectives to include political-economy and practice approaches that would make power an important missiological consideration. This study suggests that Wolf makes an important missiological contribution by advocating, "Specification of ideologies in cultural terms can only be part of our task. We must always know how these cultural forms engage with the material resources and organizational arrangements of the world they try to affect and transform" (Wolf 1999, 280).

This study would further advance the need to see modernity in all its guises as a missiological challenge (Shenk 1993). This is beginning to happen with the "Gospel and Our Culture" network moving among missiological circles. Culture has too often been regarded as a primordial homogenous essence as missiologists work with notions of inculturation, indigenization, and contextualization. Modernity is also not a fixed essence which can be relegated to the geographic West. This study demonstrates the need to rethink these concepts in the development of missiological practice and theories.

Finally, this study asserts that power needs to be a central concern in missiology. Efforts in the development of what is called "transformational development" will be helpful toward this end (Myers 1999; Christian 1999). Missiology is dominated by a concern of the relationship between gospel and culture. I would posit that the more important concern is between gospel and power. This leads then to a focus on the issue of asymmetry and injustice. Allow me to move beyond the scope of this study to make my point by reworking a primary missiological model from biblical sources.

A dominant biblical paradigm for missiological practice is incarnation, particularly from the perspective of Philippians 2:6-8, the oldest hymn in the New Testament. Missiologists predominantly focus interpretation on God becoming a Jew shaped by first century Roman-occupied Jewish culture (cultural perspective). I would suggest that this is of secondary importance on the strength of the text itself. The key to this interpretation is that God took the form of a slave (*morphē doulos*) which has to do more with power contextualized within culture. This is the self-emptying (*kenosis*) of God in a particular form that is divested of power.

My study would support this alternative reading of the incarnation and submit that an important question for missiologists to ask is where Christian theology and practice stand in relation to the powerless and poor. I will go as far as to suggest that the measure of an indigenous church, its theology and the contextualization of the gospel message, can be determined by the degree to which it meets the needs of the poor and is perceived by the poor as relevant to their lived realities. A critical missiology from this perspective seeks to envision and embody Christianity as a challenge to inequitable social relations and hegemonic regimes of power who legitimize them (state, corporation, and even church) in order to offer hope of a better life to the marginalized, oppressed, and powerless.

Afterword

LIKE ALL GOOD ETHNOGRAPHY Stephen C. Pavey's *Theologies of Power and Crisis: Envisioning/Embodying Christianity in Hong Kong* links the abstractly expressed big picture with the micro-level of lived lives. In this case the "big picture" is the world of power and politics as expressed in the unraveling and restructuring of the relationship between the United Kingdom and one of the last of its remaining colonies, Hong Kong. In this case the macro-level consists of those contemporary political players, mostly British and Chinese, associated with one of the products of the colonial era of world history. The micro-level consists of the complex and diverse lives of today's Hong Kong Christians. This research produces understanding of the processes that operated in the relationship between the political economy and theological practice associated with the 1997 "hand-over" of the British colony of Hong Kong to become part of the People's Republic of China. This transformation, negotiated between the British Government and the Chinese in 1984, ended 186 years of British control.

In contrast to the People's Republic, Hong Kong has a significant Christian population. Although smaller than Hong Kong's Buddhist and Taoist populations, the Christian population of Hong Kong is substantial. Further it is politically and economically more important than its size would suggest. Christians comprise about eight percent of the Hong Kong population, roughly half Protestant and half Roman Catholic, with some Mormons, Eastern Orthodox and others. Today's population reflects the success of the missions of various denominations starting in 1841. The establishment of the mission programs of various Christian denominations was an important tool in achieving colonial domination and ultimately making Hong Kong fit for capitalism. Beyond this the Hong Kong Christians were often important in the Hong Kong business community while they served as a link between Hong Kong and the capitalist west through both economic and religious ties. For these reasons the impact of Hong Kong Christians on Hong Kong life goes beyond their eight percent. In spite of this there has been relatively little anthropological research among the Christian communities of Hong Kong. At the same time western anthropologists had no access to the mainland. Somehow anthropologists seemed to see Hong Kong Christians as inauthentic and tended to invest their research efforts with "real" people, which in the case of Hong Kong often meant ethnic or "tribal" minorities. In fact until the "hand-over" anthropological research in Hong Kong generally was quite limited. Pavey's work is part of a new wave of interest in research among Christians in Hong Kong.

Because of the historically anti-religious, suppressive stance of the People's Republic, there was great concern about the fate of Christians in the "hand over" in spite of the assurances of religious freedom contained in the "Basic Law." According to the agreements developed between the British and the People's Republic, Hong Kong was to be administered as a semi-autonomous region which, though part of the fabric of the People's Republic was administered by special rules. These rules provided for continuation of Hong Kong's place in the capitalist world and limited government control of church life and expressions of Christianity. Pavey's work fills an important gap in this research domain.

Pavey analyzes the changing theology of Hong Kong Chinese Christians and skillfully places this in the context of the concepts and theories of Eric Wolf's precedent setting analysis, Envisioning Power. Also an anthropologist, Wolf contributes incalculably to our understanding of the global nature of the linkages between cultural groups historically in his Europe and the People without History. Succinctly expressed he demonstrates that what seemed to be culturally isolated communities have been and are linked globally. In this perspective the world is a totality of interconnected processes. In due course his analysis turned to power. Largely in the research domain of sociologists and political scientists, power is only now an increasing research interest of anthropologists. In this context, Wolf exhorts anthropologists to explore the relationships between organization and power. This is not just of theoretical interest but is at the heart of the most important issues facing the world today. In the political realm the world faces the significant risks and has incurred substantial costs because of the distortions caused by the institutions that resulted from the unequal distribution of power. This is especially apparent in the conflict expressed in the religious realm, as there is so much violence that is thought by its perpetrators as "God's work." Pavey responds to Wolf's request by focusing his attention on the associations between meaning and power in theological discourses and practices as they occurred in the context of Hong Kong Christian life. This is a difficult task because of the need to hide relationships of power in the religious domain.

The linkages between politics and the lived life that Pavey makes are more typical of contemporary anthropology than the discipline of the past. Anthropology is no longer the science of the isolated and obscure. Pavey reaches into the diverse tool kit of contemporary ethnography and uses participant observation, key informant interviewing and archival research as a foundation for his insights. This was supplemented with focus groups and structured interviews. This was all linked together with the experience of being an eyewitness.

With this work Pavey successfully extends anthropological analysis to new realms as he contributes to our understanding of Christian Asia. He demonstrates the intellectual value of ethnography in our quest to understand the world around us. It is an excellent example of anthropology engaged in the world. Perhaps this work will teach and influence those involved with cross-cultural practices in a variety of settings.

John van Willigen
Professor Emeritus of Anthropology, University of Kentucky

Bibliography

Abu-lughod, Lila. 1989. "Zones of Theory in the Anthropology of the Arab World." *Annual Review of Anthropology* 18:267–306.
Aijmer, Goran. 1967. "Expansion and Extension in Hakka Society." *Journal of the Hong Kong Branch of the Royal Asiatic Society* 7:42–79.
———. 1968. "Being Caught by a Fishnet: On Fengshui in Southeast China." *Journal of Hong Kong Branch of the Royal Asiatic Society* 8:74–81.
———. 1973. "Migrants into Hong Kong's New Territories: On the Background of Outside Vegetable Farmers." *Ethnos* 1:57–70.
———. 1980. *Economic Man in Shatin: Immigrants in a Hong Kong Valley*. London: Curzon.
———. 1986. *Atomistic Society in Sha Tin: Immigrants in a Hong Kong Valley, Gothenburg Studies in Social Anthropology 6*. Goteborg, Sweden: Acta Universitatis Gothoburgensis.
———. 1993. *Burial, Ancestors and Geomancy among the Ma on Shan Hakka, New Territories of Hong Kong, Discussions in Social Anthropology and Culture History, No. 9*. Sweden: IASSA, Göteborgs Universitet.
Althaus-Reid, Marcella. 2000. *Indecent Theology: Theological Per/Versions in Sex, Gender, and Politics*. London: Routledge.
Appadurai, Arjun. 1986. "Theory in Anthropology: Center and Periphery." *Comparative Studies in Society and History* 28:356–61.
———. 1996. *Modernity at Large: Cultural Dimensions of Globalism*. Minneapolis: University of Minnesota Press.
Apter, Andrew. 1992. *Black Critics and Kings: The Hermeneutics of Power in Yoruba Society*. Chicago: University of Chicago Press.
Asad, Talal. 1983. "Anthropological Conceptions of Religion: Reflections on Geertz." *Man* 18:237–59.
———. 1986. *The Idea of an Anthropology of Islam, Occasional Paper Series: Center of Contemporary Arabic Studies*. Washington, DC: Georgetown University Press.
———. 1993. *Genealogies of Religion: Discipline and Reasons of Power in Christianity and Islam*. Baltimore: The John Hopkins University Press.
———. 1999. "Religion, Nation-State, Secularism." In *Nation and Religion: Perspectives on Europe and Asia*, edited by Peter van der Veer and Hartmut Lehmann, 178–96. Princeton, NJ: Princeton University Press.
Baker, Hugh D. R. 1966. "The Five Great Clans of the New Territories." *Journal of the Hong Kong Branch of the Royal Asiatic Society* 6:25–48.
———. 1968. *A Chinese Lineage Village: Sheung Shui*. Stanford: Stanford University Press.
———. 1977. "Extended Kinship in the Traditional City." In *The City in Late Imperial China*, edited by G. William Skinner, 499–518. Stanford: Stanford University Press.

———. 1983. "Life in the Cities: The Emergence of Hong Kong Man." *The China Quarterly* 95:469–79.

———. 1994. *The Chop Suey Connection, Hong Kong, an Inaugural Lecture Delivered on 8 December 1993*. London: School of Oriental and African Studies, University of London.

———. 1995. "Social Change in Hong Kong: Hong Kong Man in Search of Majority." In *Greater China: The Next Superpower*, edited by David Shambaugh, 212–25. New York: Oxford University Press.

Barrett, David B., editor. 1982. *China: Indigenous Churches, World Christianity Encyclopedia*. New York: Oxford University Press.

Barrett, Stanley R., Sean Stokholm, and Jeanette Burke. 2001. "The Idea of Power and the Power of Ideas: A Review Essay." *American Anthropologist* 103:468–80.

Bax, Mart. 1985. "Popular Devotions, Power, and Religious Regimes in Catholic Dutch Brabant." *Ethnology* 24:215–27.

———. 1987. "Religious Regimes and State Formation: Towards a Research Perspective." *Anthropological Quarterly* 60:1–11.

———. 1991. "Religious Regimes and State-Formation: Toward a Research Perspective." In *Religious Regimes and State-Formation: Perspectives from European Ethnology*, edited by Eric R. Wolf, 7–28. Albany: State University of New York.

Bax, Mart, and Adrianus Koster, editors. 1993. *Power and Prayer: Religious and Political Processes in Past and Present*. Amsterdam: VU University Press.

Bays, Daniel H., editor. 1996. *Christianity in China: From the Eighteenth Century to the Present*. Stanford, CA: Stanford University Press.

Berger, Peter L. 1997. "Epistemological Modesty: An Interview with Peter Berger." *Christian Century*, 972–78.

———. 1998. "Protestantism and the Quest for Certainty." *The Christian Century*, 782–83.

———. 1999. *The Desecularization of the World: Resurgent Religion and World Politics*. Grand Rapids, MI: Eerdmans.

Berkowitz, Morris I., Frederick P. Brandauer, and John H. Reed. 1968. "Study Program on Chinese Religious Practices in Hong Kong: A Progress Report." *Ching Feng* 11:5–19.

———. 1969. *Folk Religion in an Urban Setting: A Study of Hakka Villages in Transition*. Hong Kong: Christian Study Centre on Chinese Religion and Culture.

Bernard, H. Russell. 1995. *Research Methods in Anthropology: Qualitative and Quantitative Approaches*. 2nd ed. Walnut Creek, CA: AltaMira.

Blake, Fred C. 1981. *Ethnic Groups and Social Change in a Chinese Market Town*. Honolulu: University Press of Hawaii.

Bloch, Maurice. 1989. *Ritual, History and Power: Selected Papers in Anthropology*. London: Athlone.

Boff, Clodovis. 1987. *Theology and Praxis*. Maryknoll, NY: Orbis.

Bosch, David J. 1987. "Vision for Mission." *International Review of Mission* 76:8–15.

Bourdieu, Pierre. 1993. "The Production of Belief: Contribution to an Economy of Symbolic Goods (1986)." In *The Field of Cutural Production: Essays in Art and Literature*, edited by Randal Johnson, 74–111. New York: Columbia University.

Bourdillon, M. F. C. 1993. "Anthropological Approaches to the Study of Religion." *Numen* 40:217–39.

———. 1995. "On the Theology of Anthropology: A Response to Stephen Buckland." *Studies in World Christianity* 2:45–54.

Bowie, Fiona. 1998. "Trespassing on Sacred Domains: A Feminist Anthropological Approach to Theology and Religious Studies." *Journal of Feminist Studies in Religion* 14:40–62.

———. 2000. *The Anthropology of Religion: An Introduction*. Malden, MA: Blackwell.

———. 2003. "An Anthropology of Religious Experience: Spirituality, Gender and Cultural Transmission in the Focolare Movement." *Ethnos* 68:49–72.

Brown, Deborah Ann. 1993. *Turmoil in Hong Kong on the Eve of Communist Rule: The Fate of the Territory and Its Anglican Church*. San Francisco: Mellen Research University Press.

Buckland, Stephen. 1995. "Culture and Religion as Text." *Studies in World Christianity* 2:26–44.

Budde, Michael L., and Robert W. Brimlow, editors. 2000a. *Christianity Incorporated: How Big Business Is Buying the Church*. Grand Rapids: Brazos.

———, editors. 2000b. *The Church as Counterculture*. Albany: State University of New York Press.

Burawoy, Michael, editor. 1991. *Ethnography Unbound: Power and Resistance in the Modern Metropolis*. Berkeley: University of California Press.

Carrier, James G., editor. 1997. *Meanings of Markets: The Free Market in Western Culture*. Oxford: Berg.

Carroll, John M. 1999. "Chinese Collaboration in the Making of British Hong Kong." In *Hong Kong's History: State and Society under Colonial Rule*, edited by Tak-Wing Ngo, 13–29. New York: Routledge.

Chan, Quinton. 1997. "Lutheran Church Drops Criticism of Beijing." *South China Morning Post* (July 24) 7.

Chan, Shun-hing. 1995. "The Making of Religious Universe: A Study of a Charismatic Church in Hong Kong." PhD, Chinese University of Hong Kong.

———. 1999. "Three Types of Church-State Relations in Hong Kong (in Chinese)." *Reflection* 62:4–8.

Chan, Selina Ching. 1998. "Politicizing Tradition: The Identity of Indigenous Inhabitants in Hong Kong." *Ethnology* 37:39–54.

Cheng, May M., and Siu-lun Wong. 1997. "Religious Convictions and Sentiments." In *Indicators of Social Development: Hong Kong 1995*, edited by Siu-kai Lau et al., 299–329. Hong Kong: The Chinese University of Hong Kong.

Cheng, May Ming-chun. 1998. "Familism and the Protestant Expansion in China." *Ching Feng* 41:171–97.

Chia, Philip P. 1999. "Postcolonization and Recolonization: A Response to Archie Lee's 'Biblical Interpretation in Postcolonial Hong Kong.'" *Biblical Interpretation: A Journal of Contemporary Approaches* 7:174–81.

Choi, Po-King. 1998. "The Politics of Identity: The Women's Movement in Hong Kong." *Chinese Sociology and Anthropology* 30:65–74.

Chow, John Kin-man. 1995. "'While They Are Talking of Peace and Security...': A Case for Shalom in Hong Kong." *Ching Feng* 38:287–305.

Christian, Jayakumar. 1999. *God of the Empty-Handed: Poverty, Power, and the Kingdom of God*. Monrovia, CA: MARC.

Comaroff, Jean. 1985. *Body of Power, Spirit of Resistance: The Culture and History of the South African People*. Chicago: University of Chicago Press.

———. 1994. "Defying Disenchantment: Notes on Religion, Resistance, and The 'Modern' State." In *Asian Visions of Authority: Religion and the Modern States of*

East and Southeast Asia, edited by C.F. Keyes, L. Kendall, and H. Hardacre, 301–14. Honolulu: University of Hawaii Press.

Comaroff, Jean, and John Comaroff. 1986. "Christianity and Colonialism in South Africa." *American Ethnologist* 13:1–22.

———. 1991. *Of Revelation and Reason: Christianity, Colonialism and Consciousness in South Africa*. Vol. 1. Chicago: University of Chicago Press.

———, editors. 1993. *Modernity and Its Malcontents: Ritual and Power in Post Colonial Africa*. Chicago: University of Chicago Press.

Constable, Nicole. 1988. "Fieldwork in Hong Kong." *Hong Kong Anthropological Bulletin* 2:8–10.

———. 1994. *Christian Souls and Chinese Spirits: A Hakka Community in Hong Kong*. Berkeley: University of California Press.

———. 1996. "The Negotiation of Chinese Culture in the Life of a Hakka Christian Man." *Ching Feng* 39:25–47.

Coulson, Gail V., Christopher Herlinger, and Camille S. Anders. 1996. *The Enduring Church: Christians in China and Hong Kong*. New York: Friendship.

Cunningham, Hilary. 1995. *God and Caesar at the Rio Grande: Sanctuary and the Politics of Religion*. Minneapolis: University of Minnesota Press.

Dilley, Roy, editor. 1992. *Contesting Markets: Analysis of Ideology, Discourse and Practice*. Edinburgh: Edinburgh University Press, 1992.

Douglas, Mary. 1982. "The Effects of Modernization on Religious Change." *Daedalus* 111:1–20.

Dube, Saurabh. 1998. *Untouchable Pasts: Religion, Identity, and Power among a Central Indian Community, 1780–1950*. Albany: State University of New York.

el-Zein, Abdul Hamid. 1977. "Beyond Ideology and Theology: The Search for an Anthropology of Islam." *Annual Review of Anthropology* 6:227–54.

Evans, Grant, and Siu-mi Maria Tam. 1997. *Hong Kong: The Anthropology of a Chinese Metropolis*. Richmond, Surrey: Curzon.

Evans-Pritchard, E. E. 1956a. "Religion." In *The Institutions of Primitive Society*, Glencoe, IL: Free Press.

———. 1956b. *Nuer Religion*. Oxford, Oxford University Press.

———. 1960. "Introduction." In *Death and the Right Hand* by R. Hertz, translated by Rodney and Claudia Needham, 9–24. London: Cohen & West.

———. 1965. *Theories of Primitive Religion*. Oxford: Oxford University Press.

———. 1972. "Religion and Anthropologists." *Practical Anthropology* 19:193–206.

———. 1981. *A History of Anthropological Thought*. New York: Basic Books.

Evens, T. M. S. 1982. "On the Social Anthropology of Religion." *The Journal of Religion* 62:376–91.

Ewing, Katherine Pratt. 1994. "Dreams from a Saint: Anthropological Atheism and the Temptation to Believe." *American Anthropologist* 96:571 83.

Faure, David. 1986. *The Structure of Chinese Rural Society: Lineage and Village in the Eastern New Territories*. Hong Kong: Oxford University Press.

———. 1989a. "The Lineage as a Cultural Invention: The Case of the Pearl River Delta." *Modern China* 15:4–36.

———. 1989b. "Folk Religion in Hong Kong and the New Territories Today." In *The Turning of the Tide: Religion in China Today*, edited by Julian F. Pas, 259–74. Hong Kong: Royal Asiatic Society, Hong Kong Branch, in association with Oxford University Press.

———, ed. 1995. *History of Hong Kong 1842–1984*. Hong Kong: Tamarind.
———. 1997. "Reflections on Being Chinese in Hong Kong." In *Hong Kong's Transitions, 1842–1997*, edited by Judith M. Brown and Rosemary Foot, 103–20. St. Anthony's Series. London: MacMillan.
Faure, David, James Hayes, and Alan Birch, editors. 1984. *From Village to City: Studies in the Traditional Roots of Hong Kong Society*. Hong Kong: Centre of Asian Studies, The University of Hong Kong.
Faure, David, and Tao Tao Liu, editors. 1996. *Unity and Diversity: Local Cultures and Identities in China*. Hong Kong: Hong Kong University Press.
Feng, Ren-zhao. 1998. "The Hongkongese: Who Are the Hongkongnese?" *Chinese Sociology and Anthropology* 30:37–44.
Firth, Raymond. 1981. "Spiritual Aroma: Religion and Politics." *American Anthropologist* 83:582–601.
Foucault, Michel. 1980. *Power/Knowledge: Selected Interviews and Other Writings, 1972–1977*. Translated by Colin Gordon. New York: Pantheon.
Freedman, Maurice. 1966. "Shifts of Power in the Hong Kong New Territories." *Journal of Asian and African Studies* 1.1:3–12.
———. 1976. "A Report on Social Research in the New Territories, 1963." 16:191–261.
———. 1979. "Chinese Geomancy: Some Observations in Hong Kong." In *The Study of Chinese Society*, 189–211. Stanford, CA: Stanford University Press.
Freedman, Maurice, Stephan Feuchtwang, and Hugh D. R. Baker, editors. 1991. *An Old State in New Settings: Studies in the Social Anthropology of China in Memory of Maurice Freedman, Jaso Occasional Papers, No. 8*. Oxford: JASO.
Fung, Raymond. 1977. "On Doing Theology in Asia: An Industrial Missioner's Reflections on the Manilla Theological Consultation." *Ching Feng* 20:148–52.
Gardner, Katy, and David Lewis. 1996. *Anthropology, Development and the Post-Modern Challenge*. London: Pluto.
Geertz, Clifford. 1973. *The Interpretation of Cultures: Selected Essays*. New York: Basic Books.
———. 2000. "The Pinch of Destiny: Religion as Experience, Meaning, Identity, Power." In *Available Light: Anthropological Reflections on Philosophical Topics*, 167–86. Princeton: Princeton University Press.
Ghani, Ashraf. 1987. "A Conversation with Eric Wolf." *American Ethnologist* 14:346–67.
Glazier, Stephen D., editor. 1997. *Anthropology of Religion: A Handbook*. Westport, CT: Greenwood.
———. 2000. "Anthropology and Theology: The Legacy of a Link." In *Anthropology and Theology: Gods, Icons, and God-Talk*, edited by Frank A. Salamone, 407–20. Lanham, MD: University Press of America.
Goodman, Alan H., and Thomas L. Leatherman, editors. 1998. *Building a New Biocultural Synthesis: Political-Economic Perspectives on Human Biology*. Ann Arbor: University of Michigan Press.
Goodman, Felicitas. 1991. "The Discomfiture of Religious Experience." *Religion* 21:339–44.
Graeber, David. 2001. *Towards an Anthropological Theory of Value: The False Coin of Our Own Dreams*. New York: Palgrave.
Granberg, Hakan. 2000. *Church Planting Commitment: New Church Development in Hong Kong During the Run-up to 1997*. Finland: Abo Akademi University Press.

Groves, Robert. 1964. "The Origins of Two Market Towns in the New Territories." In *Aspects of Social Organization in the New Territories*, edited by Marjorie Topley, 16–20. Hong Kong: Cathay.

———. 1969. "Militia, Market and Lineage: Chinese Resistance to the Occupation of the New Territories in 1899." *Journal of the Hong Kong Branch of the Royal Asiatic Society* 9:31–64.

Guldin, Gregory E. 1977a. "Little Fujian (Fukien) Sub-Neighborhood and Community in North Point, Hong Kong." *Journal of the Hong Kong Branch of the Royal Asiatic Society*, 112–19.

———. 1977b. "Overseas at Home: The Fujianese of Hong Kong." PhD diss., University of Wisconsin-Madison.

———. 1982. "Whose Neighborhood Is This? Ethnicity and Community in Hong Kong." *Urban Anthropology* 9:243–63.

Ha, Seong-kwong Louis. 1991. "Catholicism in Hong Kong." In *The Other Hong Kong Report 1991*, edited by Yun-wing Sung and Ming-kwan Lee, 527–41. Hong Kong: Chinese University Press.

Harding, Susan. 1987. "Convicted by the Holy Spirit: The Rhetoric of Fundamental Baptist Conversion." *American Ethnologist* 14:167–82.

———. 1988. "*Review of* God's Choice: The Total World of a Fundamentalist Christian School." *American Ethnologist* 15:582.

———. 1991. "Representing Fundamentalism: The Problem of the Repugnant Cultural Other." *Social Research* 58:373–93.

———. 2000. *The Book of Jerry Falwell: Fundamentalist Language and Politics*. Princeton: Princeton University Press.

Hong Kong Christian Council (HKCC), editor. 1982. *The Churches in Hong Kong and the Future of Hong Kong (in Chinese)*. Hong Kong: Hong Kong Christian Council.

———. 1984. "A Manifesto of the Protestant Church in Hong Kong on Religious Freedom." Hong Kong: Hong Kong Christian Council.

———. 1986. "The Mission of the Church in Hong Kong: A Report of the Mid-Decade Mission." Consultation, January 19–22, 1986." Hong Kong: Hong Kong Christian Council.

Hong Kong Church Renewal Movement (HKCRM), editor. 2000. *1999 Hong Kong Church Survey (in Chinese)*. Hong Kong: Hong Kong Church Renewal Movement.

Hong Kong Evangelical Christian Leaders. 1984. "The Convictions Held by Christians in Hong Kong in the Midst of Contemporary Social and Political Change." In *Hong Kong Church and 1997: Historical Documents of the Hong Kong Church Response to 1997*, 5–8. Compiled by Hong Kong Christian Council. Online: http://www.hkcc.org.hk/database/declarations/HONG%20KONG%20CHURCH%20and%201997.pdf.

Hon, May Sin-mi. 2001. "Charity Warned over Political Acts." *South China Morning Post* (February 5).

Hughes, Richard. 1976. *Borrowed Place Borrowed Time: Hong Kong and Its Many Faces*. 2nd ed. London: Andre Deutsch.

Hui, C. Harry. 1991. "Religious and Supernaturalistic Beliefs." In *Indicators of Social Development: Hong Kong 1988*, edited by Siu-kai Lau, 103–43. Hong Kong: Hong Kong Institute of Asia-Pacific Studies, Chinese University of Hong Kong.

Karsen, Wendell. 1980. "The Church and Education in Hong Kong." *News and Views* (September) 6–8.

Kaung, Joseph Tai-wai, editor. 1985. *Christianity and Politics—in the Hong Kong Context (in Chinese)*. Tolo Theological Series 3. Hong Kong: Chung Chi College Theological Division.

———. 1993. "Theological Decolonization: A Commentary on 1997." *News and Views* (March) 17–22.

———. 1994. "The Decolonization of Theology (in Chinese)." In *Invitation to Theology*, edited by Shun-hing Chan, 249–70. Hong Kong: Hong Kong Christian Institute.

———. 1996. "A Hong Kong Response to Chhut-Thau-Thi Theology." *Ching Feng* 39:115–18.

———. 2003. "The Middle Class Cum Middle-Aged Crisis." *Hong Kong Christian Institute Newsletter* 174 (March). Online: http://www.hkci.org.hk/eng/newsletter/174a.html.

Kaung, Joseph Tai-wai, and Yee Wah Lau, editors. 1999. *Politics and the Christian (in Chinese)*. Hong Kong: Chung Chi College Theological Division.

Kertzer, David. 1988. *Ritual, Politics, and Power*. New Haven, CT: Yale University Press.

King, Ambrose Y. C., editor. 1981. *Social Life and Development in Hong Kong*. Hong Kong: The Chinese University Press.

Ko, Tin-ming. 1998. "The Sacred Citizens and the Secular City: A Study of the Political Participation of Protestant Ministers in Hong Kong." PhD, City University of Hong Kong.

———. 2000. *The Sacred Citizens and the Secular City: Political Participation of Protestant Ministers in Hong Kong*. Aldershot: Ashgate.

Koyama, Kosuke. 1974. *Water Buffalo Theology*. Maryknoll, NY: Orbis.

Kung, Lap-yan. 1995. "The Cultural Dimension of Liberation Theology: The Case of Hong Kong." *Ching Feng* 38:213–26.

Kwan, Choi Wah. 1996. *The Right Word in Cantonese*. Hong Kong: Commercial.

Kwan, Simon Shui-man. 1998. "An Introduction to the Hong Kong Context and Its Theologies." Paper given at 1996 Youth Conference of the CCA on Reading the Bible through Asian Eyes, March 12–20, 1996, at Nanjing Theological Seminary. In *Report on Reading the Bible through Asian Eyes, Nanjing, China, CCA Youth Conference*, edited by Ngan-ling Lung, no pages. Hong Kong: CCA Youth.

———. 1999a. "Asian Critical Hermeneutics Amidst the Economic Development of Asia." *Asia Journal of Theology* 13:354–74.

———. 1999b. "Collaboration as an Alternative Mode of Anti-Colonialist Resistance: A Postcolonial of the Asia-West Binarism Inscribed in the Asian Theological Movement." PhD diss., Chinese University of Hong Kong.

Kwok, Nai-wang. 1991. *Hong Kong 1997: A Christian Perspective*. Hong Kong: Urban Rural Mission, Christian Conference of Asia.

———. 1994. *Hong Kong Braves 1997*. Edited by Loren Keith Stanton. Hong Kong: Hong Kong Christian Institute.

———. 1996. *1997: Hong Kong's Struggle for Selfhood*. Hong Kong: Daga.

———. 1997a. "Christian Churches in Hong Kong under Colonial Rule." *Tripod* 17:28–42.

———. 1997b. *A Church in Transition*. Hong Kong: Hong Kong Christian Institute.

Kwok, Pui-lan. 1995. *Discovering the Bible in the Non-Biblical World*. Maryknoll, NY: Orbis.

Kwong, Chun-wah. 2000. *Hong Kong's Religions in Transition*. Waco, TX: Tao Foundation.

Lambek, Michael. 2000. "The Anthropology of Religion and the Quarrel between Poetry and Philosophy." *Current Anthropology* 41:309–20.

Lang, Graeme, and Lars Ragvald. 1988. "Upward Mobility of a Refugee God: Hong Kong's Huang Daxian." *The Stockholm Journal of East Asian Studies* 1:54–87.

———. 1993. *The Rise of a Refugee God: Hong Kong's Wong Tai Sin*. Hong Kong: Oxford University Press.

Lau, Emily. 1987. "An Unholy Alliance: Protestant Liberals Accuse Leaders of Bowing to Peking." *Far Eastern Economic Review* 24:23.

Lau, Siu-kai. 1982. *Society and Politics in Hong Kong*. Hong Kong: The Chinese University Press.

Lau, Siu-kai, and Hsin-chi Kuan. 1988. *The Ethos of the Hong Kong People*. Hong Kong: Chinese University Press.

Law, Gail, editor. 1982. *Chinese Churches Handbook*. Hong Kong: Chinese Coordination Centre of World Evangelism.

Lee, Archie Chi-chung. 1980. "The Torah Story and the Mission of the Church in Hong Kong in the Eighties." Paper presented at The Mission of the Church in Hong Kong in the Eighties, Hong Kong.

———. 1982. "The Churches of Hong Kong and the Future of Hong Kong: The Issue of Identity." In *The Churches in Hong Kong and the Future of Hong Kong*, edited by HKCC, no pages. Hong Kong: Hong Kong Christian Council.

———. 1991. "The David-Bathsheba Story and the Parable of Nathan." In *Voices from the Margin: Interpreting the Bible in the Third World*, edited by R. S. Sugirtharajah, 189–204. Maryknoll, NY: Orbis.

———. 1992. *Hong Kong's Transition to 1997: Christian Responses to Confidence Crisis*: The ILIFF Week of Lectures. Cassette.

———. 1993a. "Biblical Interpretation in Asian Perspective." *Asia Journal of Theology* 7:35–39.

———. 1993b. "Genesis 1 from the Perspective of a Chinese Creation Myth." In *Understanding Poets and Prophets*, edited by A. Graeme Auld, 186–98. Sheffield: Sheffield Academic Press.

———. 1994a. "Biblical Precedence in Contextualizing Local Festivals and Customs." In *Doing Theology with the Festivals and Customs of Asia*, 1–10. Singapore: ATESEA.

———. 1994b. "The Chinese Creation Myth of Nu Kua and the Biblical Narrative in Genesis 1–11." *Biblical Interpretation* 2:312–24.

———. 1995. "Exile and Return in the Perspective of 1997." In *Reading from This Place: Social Location and Biblical Interpretation in Global Perspective*, edited by F. F. Segovia and M. A. Tolbert, 97–108. Minneapolis, MN: Fortress.

———, editor. 1996a. *The Asian Context and Biblical Hermeneutics (in Chinese)*. Hong Kong: Chinese Christian Literature Council.

———. 1996b. "Cross Textual Hermeneutics on Gospel and Culture." *Asian Journal of Theology* 10:38–48.

———. 1996c. "Syncretism from the Perspectives of Chinese Religion and Biblical Tradition." *Ching Feng* 29:1–24.

———. 1997. "Reclaiming Asian Resources for Christian Theology in Asia." *PTCA Bulletin* 10:1–4.

———. 1999a. "Returning to China: Biblical Interpretation in Postcolonial Hong Kong." *Biblical Interpretation* 7:156–73.

———. 1999b. "Identity, Reading Strategy and Doing Theology." *Biblical Interpretation* 7:187–201.
———. 1999c. *Texts and Interpretation: Contemporary Meaning of the Old Testament (in Chinese)*. Hong Kong: Hong Kong Christian Institute.
Lee-Young, Joanne. 2000. "A New Church on the Block." *The Asian Wall Street Journal* (February 18–19) 1–4.
Leung, Beatrice. 1998. "Church-State Relations in the Decolonisation Period: Hong Kong and Macau." *Religion, State & Society* 26:17–30.
Leung, Beatrice, and John D. Young, editors. 1997. *Christianity in China: Foundations for Dialogue*. Centre of Asian Studies: The University of Hong Kong.
Leung, Ka-lun. 1999. "The Minority and a Minority Attitude." *Jian Dao* 12:161–90.
Levi-Strauss, Claude. 1966. "The Scope of Anthropology." *Current Anthropology* 7:112–23.
Levy-Bruhl, Lucien. 1923. *Primitive Mentality*. New York.
———. 1926. *How Natives Think*. London.
———. 1928. *The "Soul" of the Primitive*. New York.
Li, Kin-wah. 1999. *Blood Is Thicker Than Water: Handbook for Caring for New Arrivals* (in Chinese). Hong Kong: Mission to New Arrivals.
Li, Kin-wah, and Siu-han Catherine Lee, editors. 1996. *Xiangang Jiaohui Weilai Qushi (Trends and the Future of Hong Kong Churches: Findings of 1994 Survey)*. Hong Kong: World Vision HK.
Lienhardt, Godfrey. 1968. "Primitive Theology." In *International Encyclopedia of the Social Sciences*, edited by David L. Sills, 15:604–8. New York: Macmillan.
Lilley, Rozanna. 1993. "Claiming Identity: Film and Television in Hong Kong." *History and Anthropology* 6:261–92.
———. 1996. "Playing the Moment: The Conditional Present in Hong Kong." *Anthropological Notebooks* 2:55–75.
Liu, Agnes Tat-fong. 1996a. "Conversion of the Urban Poor." In *Sharing the Good News with the Poor: A Reader for Concerned Christians*, edited by Bruce J. Nicholls and Beulah R. Wood, 230–40. Grand Rapids: Baker.
———. 1996b. "Training the Poor for Ministry to the Poor." In *Sharing the Good News with the Poor: A Reader for Concerned Christians*, edited by Bruce J. Nicholls and Beulah R. Wood, 279–83. Grand Rapids: Baker.
———. 1999. "Negotiating Social Status: Religion and Ethnicity in a Seui Seuhng Yahn Settlement in Hong Kong." PhD diss., Chinese University of Hong Kong.
Lo, Lung-kwong. 1997. "The Future of the Church in Hong Kong." *Word and World* 17:203–11.
Luk, Bernard H. K. 1990. "Custom and Religion." In *The Other Hong Kong Report*, edited by Richard Y.C. Wong and Joseph Y.S. Cheng, 565–81. Hong Kong: The Chinese University of Hong Kong.
Lyon, Robert W. n.d. "The Poor Church as the Truly Evangelic Church." Asbury Theological Seminary. Unpublished paper.
———. 1986. "Abandoning Power: The L.O. Society at Asbury Theological Seminary." In *Transformation: An International Journal of Holistic Mission Studies* 3:10–13.
Ma, Eddie Kin-ming. 1997. "Hong Kong and the 1997 Crisis: Danger or Opportunity? Strategies for Baptist Mission and Growth in a Climate of Political Transition." DMiss diss., Asbury Theological Seminary.

Madsen, Richard. 1998. *China's Catholics: Tragedy and Hope in an Emerging Civil Society*. Berkeley: University of California Press.

Mak, Sai-king. 1991. "Church Governance." MBA thesis, University of Hong Kong.

Man, Si-wai, and Sze-ping Lo. 1998. "Guest Editors' Introduction: Cultural Identity." *Chinese Sociology and Anthropology* 30:3–12.

Mark, Timothy. 1998. "A Tale of China's Two Churches." *Christianity Today* 42:30.

Mathews, Gordon. 1996. "Names and Identities in the Hong Kong Cultural Supermarket." *Dialectical Anthropology* 21:399–419.

———. 1997. "Heunggongyahn: On the Past, Present, and Future of Hong Kong Identity." *Bulletin of Concerned Asian Scholars* 29:3–13.

———. 1998. "Culture, State, and the Market in the Shaping of Hong Kong's Chinese Identity." *The Hong Kong Anthropologist* 11:22–27.

Merwin, Wallace C. 1974. *Adventure in Unity: The Church of Christ in China*. Grand Rapids: Eerdmans.

Mitchell, Robert. 1974. "Religion among Urban Chinese and Non-Chinese in Southeast Asian Countries." *Social Compass* 21:25–44.

Mufson, Steven. 1998. "U.S. Religious Leaders Tread Softly in China: Panel Meets Only with State-Approved Groups." *Washington Post* (February 19) A-21.

Myers, Bryant L. 1999. *Walking with the Poor: Principles and Practices of Transformational Development*. Maryknoll, NY: Orbis.

Myers, John T. 1976. "The "Gaau Yauh" Of Block 18: Religious Change in a Hong Kong Resettlement Estate." PhD diss., University of Pittsburgh.

———. 1981. "Traditional Chinese Religious Practices in an Urban-Industrial Setting: The Example of Kwun Tong." In *Social Life and Development in Hong Kong*, edited by Ambrose Y. C. King and Rance P. L. Lee, 275–88. Hong Kong: The Chinese University of Hong Kong.

Nader, Laura. 1969. "Up the Anthropologist—Perspectives Gained from Studying Up." In *Reinventing Anthropology*, edited by Dell Hymes, 284–311. New York: Pantheon.

Ngo, Tak-Wing, editor. 1999. *Hong Kong's History: State and Society under Colonial Rule*. Edited by Mark Selden, *Asia's Transformations*. New York: Routledge.

Norbeck, Edward. 1961. *Religion and Primitive Society*. New York: Harper & Row.

Ong, Aihwa. 1988. "The Production of Possession: Spirits and the Multinational Corporation in Malaysia." *American Ethnologist* 15:28–42.

———. 1990. "State Versus Islam: Malay Families, Women's Bodies, and the Body Politic of Malaysia." *American Ethnologist* 17:258–76.

———. 1995. "Comments on Roy D'andrade's 'Moral Models in Anthropology' And Nancy Scheper-Hughes's 'The Primacy of the Ethical: Propositions for a Militant Anthropology.'" *Current Anthropology* 36.3 (June) 428–30.

———. 1999. *Flexible Citizenship: The Cultural Logics of Transnationality*. Durham, NC: Duke University Press.

Ortner, Sherry. 1978. *Sherpas through Their Rituals*. Cambridge: Cambridge University Press.

———. 1989. *High Religion: A Cultural and Political History of Sherpa Buddhism*. Princeton: Princeton University Press.

Pandian, Jacob. 1991. *Culture, Religion, and the Sacred Self: A Critical Introduction to the Anthropological Study of Religion*. Englewood Cliffs, NJ: Prentice Hall.

———. 2001. "The Dangerous Quest for Cooperation between Science and Religion." *Skeptical Inquirer* 25 (Sept/Oct) 28–33.

———. 2002. "Anthropology and the Invention of Religion." *Anthropology Newsletter* 43:11.
Parry, Jonathan, and Maurice Bloch, editors. 1989. *Money and the Morality of Exchange*. New York: Cambridge University Press.
Paulson, Susan, Lisa L. Gezon, and Michael Watts. 2003. "Locating the Political in Political Ecology: An Introduction." *Human Organization* 62:205–17.
Pelto, Pertti J., and Gretel H. Pelto. 1978. *Anthropological Research: The Structure of Inquiry*. Cambridge: Cambridge University Press.
Poewe, Karla, editor. 1994. *Charismatic Christianity as a Global Culture*. Columbia: University of South Carolina Press.
Potter, Jack M. 1964. "Ping Shan: The Changing Economy of a Chinese Village in Hong Kong." PhD, University of California.
———. 1968. *Capitalism and the Chinese Peasant: Social and Economic Change in a Hong Kong Village*. Berkeley: University of California Press.
———. 1969. "The Structure of Rural Chinese Society in New Territories." In *Hong Kong: A Society in Transition*, edited by Ian C. Jarvie and Joseph Agassi, 3–28. Hong Kong: Centre of Asian Studies, University of Hong Kong.
Quarles van Ufford, Philip, and Matthew Schoffeleers, editors. 1988. *Religion and Development: Towards an Integrated Approach*. Amsterdam: Free University Press.
Rappaport, Roy A. 1993. "The Anthropology of Trouble." *American Anthropologist* 95:295–303.
———. 1994. "Disorders of Our Own." In *Diagnosing America: Anthropology and Public Engagement*, edited by Shepard Forman, 235–94. Ann Arbor: University of Michigan Press.
———. 1999. *Ritual and Religion in the Making of Humanity*, Cambridge Studies in Social and Cultural Studies 110. Cambridge: Cambridge University Press.
Reidhead, Van A, and Mary Ann Reidhead. 1998. "Relevance in the Anthropology of Religion." *Anthropology Newsletter* 39:35–36.
Richardson, Miles. 1975. "Anthropologist—the Myth Teller." *American Anthropologist* 2:517–33.
Robbins, Joel, and David Akin, editors. 1999. *Money and Modernity: State and Local Currencies in Melanesia*. Pittsburg: University of Pittsburg Press.
Rosaldo, Renato. 1988. "Ideology, Place, and People without Culture." *Cultural Anthropology* 3.1:77–87.
———. 1989. *Culture and Truth: The Remaking of Social Analysis*. Boston: Beacon.
Rosecrance, Richard. 1999. *The Rise of the Virtual State: Wealth and Power in the Coming Century*. New York: Basic Books.
Sahlins, Marshall. 1981. *Historical Metaphors and Mythical Realities: Structure in the Early History of the Sandwich Islands Kingdom*. Ann Arbor: University of Michigan Press.
———. 1985. *Islands of History*. Chicago: University of Chicago Press.
Salaff, Janet W. 1974. "Modern Times in Hong Kong." *Bulletin of Concerned Asian Scholars* 6:2–7.
———. 1981. *Working Daughters of Hong Kong: Filial Piety or Power in the Family?* Cambridge: Cambridge University Press.
Saler, Benson. 1993. *Conceptualizing Religion: Immanent Anthropologists, Transcendent Natives, and Unbound Categories*. Leiden: Brill.
———. 2002. "The Future of the Anthropology of Religion: Part Two." *Anthropology News* 43:52–53.

San, Wei-sze. 1987. "Basic Law and Religious Freedom." *News and Views* (April) 3–6.
Scheper-Hughes, Nancy. 1992. *Death without Weeping: The Violence of Everyday Life in Brazil.* Berkeley: University of California Press.
Schneider, Jane, and Shirley Lindenbaum. 1987. "Frontiers of Christian Evangelism: Essays in Honor of Joyce Riegelhaupt." *American Ethnologist* 14:1–8.
Schneider, Jane and Rayna Rapp, editor. 1995. *Articulating Hidden Histories: Exploring the Influence of Eric R. Wolf.* Berkeley: University of California Press.
Schoffeleers, Matthew. 1985. "Introduction: Meaning and Power—Contemporary Currents in Religious Anthropology." *Social Compass* 32:5–13.
Shaw, Rosalind. 1995. "Feminist Anthropology and the Gendering of Religious Studies." In *Religion and Gender*, edited by Ursula King. Oxford: Blackwell, 1995.
Shenk, Wilbert. 1993. "The Culture of Modernity as a Missionary Challenge." In *The Good News of the Kingdom: Mission Theology in the Third Millenium*, edited by Charles Van Engen, Dean S. Gilliland, and Paul Pierson, 192–99. Maryknoll, NY: Orbis, 1993.
Siu, Helen F. 1988. "Immigrants and Social Ethos: Hong Kong in the Nineteen-Eighties." *Journal of the Hong Kong Branch of the Royal Asiatic Society* 26:1–16.
———. 1993. "Cultural Identity and the Politics of Difference in South China." *Daedalus* 122:19–43.
———. 1996. "Remade in Hong Kong: Weaving into the Chinese Cultural Tapestry." In *Unity and Diversity: Local Cultures and Identities in China*, edited by David Faure and Tao Tao Liu. Hong Kong: Hong Kong University Press.
———. 1997. "Remade in Hong Kong." *Index on Censorship* 26:145–51.
Smart, Alan. 1985. "The Squatter Property Market in Hong Kong." *Critique of Anthropology* 5.3:23–40.
———. 1992. *Making Room: Squatter Clearance in Hong Kong.* Hong Kong: Centre of Asian Studies, University of Hong Kong.
———. 1995. "Hong Kong's Slums and Squatter Areas: A Developmental Perspective." In *Housing the Urban Poor*, edited by B. Aldrich and R. Sanhu, 97–111. London: Zed.
———. 2001. "Unruly Places: Urban Governance and the Persistence of Illegality in Hong Kong's Urban Squatter Areas." *American Anthropologist* 103.1:30–44.
Smart, Josephine. 1989. *The Political Economy of Street Hawkers in Hong Kong, Centre of Asian Studies Occasional Papers and Monographs, 81.* Hong Kong: Centre of Asian Studies, University of Hong Kong.
Smith, Carl T. 1970. "The Chinese Settlement of British Hong Kong." *Chung Chi Bulletin* 48:26–27.
———. 1985. *The Chinese Christians: Elites, Middlemen, and the Church in Hong Kong.* New York: Oxford University Press.
South China Morning Post. 1970a. "Don't Meddle in Politics, Church Leaders Told." January 20.
———. 1970b. "Churches Told to Get Closer to the People." January 21.
Stipe, Claude E. 1980. "Anthropologists Versus Missionaries: The Influence of Presuppositions." *Current Anthropology* 21:165–68.
Stirrat, R. L. 1992. *Power and Religiousity in a Post-Colonial Setting: Sinahala Catholics in Contemporary Sri Lanka.* New York: Cambridge University Press.
Tanner, Kathryn. 1994. "The Difference Theological Anthropology Makes." *Theology Today* 50:567–79.

Topley, Marjorie. 1964. "Capital, Saving and Credit among Indigenous Rice Farmers and Immigrant Vegetable Farmers in Hong Kong's New Territories." In *Capital, Saving and Credit in Peasant Societies*, edited by Raymond Firth and B. S. Yamey, 157–86. Chicago: Aldine.

———, editor. 1966. *Some Traditional Chinese Ideas and Conceptions in Hong Kong Social Life Today*. Hong Kong: Hong Kong Branch of the Royal Asiatic Society.

———. 1969. *Anthropology and Sociology in Hong Kong: Field Projects and Problems of Overseas Scholars*. Hong Kong: Centre of Asian Studies, University of Hong Kong.

Trench, Sir David. 1970. "Address to the Consultation on the Mission of the Church." Hong Kong, January 20.

Turner, Edith L. B. 1997a. "Religion and Culture in Present-Day Anthropology." *Anthropology Newsletter* (October) 38.

———. 1997b. "Religion and Culture in Present-Day Anthropology, Part 2—Characteristics of the Religious Mode: Further Work in Progress." *Anthropology Newsletter* (November) 35–36.

van der Veer, Peter, editor. 1996. *Conversion to Modernities: The Globalization of Christianity*. New York: Routledge.

van der Veer, Peter, and Hartmut Lehmann, editors. 1999. *Nation and Religion: Perspectives on Europe and Asia*. Princeton: Princeton University Press.

Verdery, Katherine. 1991. "Theorizing Socialism: A Prologue to the 'Transition.'" *American Ethnologist* 18:419–39.

Volf, Miroslav. 1996. "Theology, Meaning, and Power." In *The Future of Theology: Essays in Honor of Jürgen Moltmann*, edited by Miroslav Volf, 98–113. Grand Rapids: Eerdmans.

Wagner, Melinda Bollar. 1997. "The Study of Religion in American Society." In *Anthropology of Religion: A Handbook*, edited by Stephen D. Glazier, 85–101. Westport, CT: Greenwood.

Ward, Barbara E. 1954. "A Hong Kong Fishing Village." *Journal of Oriental Studies* 1:195–214.

———. 1959. "Floating Villages: Chinese Fisherman in Hong Kong." *Man* 59:44–45.

———. 1965. "Varieties of the Conscious Model: The Fishermen of South China." In *The Relevance of Models for Social Anthropology*, edited by Michael Banton, 113–37. Association of Social Anthropologists Monographs I. London: Tavistock.

Wark, Andrew. 1995. "Countdown to Communism: Churches in Hong Kong Fear Threat to Religious Freedom When China's Rule Returns." *Christianity Today* 39:54–61.

Watson, James L. 1972. "A Chinese Emigrant Community: The Man Lineage in Hong Kong and London." PhD diss., University of California.

———. 1975. *Emigration and the Chinese Lineage: The Mans in Hong Kong and London*. Berkeley: University of California Press.

———, editor. 1977. *Between Two Cultures: Migrants and Minorities in Britain*. Oxford: Blackwell.

———. 1983. "Rural Society: Hong Kong's New Territories." *The China Quarterly* 95:480–90.

———. 1991. *The Renegotiation of Chinese Cultural Identity in the Post-Mao Era*. Hong Kong: University of Hong Kong, Social Sciences Research Centre.

———. 1997. "McDonald's in Hong Kong: Consumerism, Dietary Change, and the Rise of a Children's Culture." In *Golden Arches East: McDonald's in East Asia*, edited by James L. Watson, 77–109. Stanford: Stanford University Press.

———. 1998. "Living Ghosts: Long-Haired Destitutes in Colonial Hong Kong." In *Hair: Its Power and Meaning in Asian Cultures*, edited by Barbara D. Miller and Alf Hiltebeitel, 177–93. Albany: State University of New York Press.

Watson, James L., and Rubie S. Watson. 1997. "From Hall of Worship to Tourist Center: An Ancestral Hall in Hong Kong's New Territories." *Cultural Survival Quarterly* 12:33–35.

Wax, Murray L. 1984. "Religion as Universal: Tribulations of an Anthropological Enterprise." *Zygon: Journal of Religion and Science* 19:5–20.

Wolf, Eric R. 1982. *Europe and the People without History*. Berkeley: University of California Press.

———, editor. 1984. *Religion, Power and Protest in Local Communities: The Northern Shore of the Mediterranean*. Religion and Society 24. Berlin: Mouton.

———. 1986. "The Vicissitudes of the Closed Corporate Peasant Community." *American Ethnologist* 13:325–29.

———. 1990. "Distinguished Lecture: Facing Power—Old Insights, New Questions." *American Anthropologist* 92:586–96.

———, editor. 1991. *Religious Regimes and State-Formation: Perspectives from European Ethnology*. Albany: State University of New York Press.

———. 1994. "Perilous Ideas: Race, Culture, People." *Current Anthropology* 35:1–12.

———. 1999. *Envisioning Power: Ideologies of Dominance and Crisis*. Berkeley: University of California Press.

———. 2001. *Pathways of Power: Building an Anthropology of the Modern World*. Berkeley: University of California Press.

Wong, Martin. 2000a. "Rich and Poor Growing Apart." *South China Morning Post* (June 22).

———. 2000b. "Income Gap Widens to Put 1.24 Million into Poverty." *South China Morning Post* (September 26).

———. 2000c. "Poor People Lazy and a Burden: Poll." *South China Morning Post* (October 6).

———. 2000d. "Poorest Suffering as Income Gap Widens." *South China Morning Post* (July 20).

———. 2000e. "Public Attitude a Barrier to Easing Plight." *South China Morning Post* (October 7).

Wong, Siu-lun. 1986. "Modernization and Chinese Culture in Hong Kong." *China Quarterly* 106:306–25.

Wong, Thomas W.P. 1998. *Colonial Goverance and the Hong Kong Story, Occasional Paper No. 77*. Hong Kong: Hong Kong Institute of Asia-Pacific Studies, The Chinese University of Hong Kong.

Wong, Thomas W.P., and Tai-lok Lui. 1993. *Morality, Class and the Hong Kong Way of Life, Occasional Paper No.30*. Hong Kong: Hong Kong Institute of Asia-Pacific Studies, The Chinese University of Hong Kong.

Wong, Wai-ching Angela. 1997a. "'The Poor Woman': A Critical Analysis of Asian Theology and Contemporary Chinese Fiction by Women." PhD diss., The University of Chicago.

———. 1997b. "Asian Theology in a Changing Asia: Towards an Asian Theological Agenda for the 21st Century." Paper presented at the Proceedings of The Congress of Asian Theologians, Part 1, 25 May 25—June 1, 1997, Suwon, Korea.

———. 1999. "History, Identity and a Community of Hesed: A Biblical Reflection on Ruth 1:1–17." *Asian Journal of Theology* 13:3–13.
Woo, Peter Kwong-ching. 1999. "Our One-Issue Town." *South China Morning Post* (December 28).
Wuthnow, Robert. 1996. *Christianity and Civil Society: The Contemporary Debate.* Valley Forge, PA: Trinity.
Xue, Zheng. 1996. "Religions in Hong Kong Facing 1997." Chinese Academy of Social Sciences. Unpublished report.
Yanagisako, Sylvia, and Carol Delaney, editors. 1995. *Naturalizing Power: Essays in Feminist Cultural Analysis.* New York: Routledge.
Ye, Xiao-wen. 1996. "The RAB Director-General's Address." *News and Views* (September) 9–10.

www.ingramcontent.com/pod-product-compliance
Lightning Source LLC
Chambersburg PA
CBHW070917160426
43193CB00011B/1501